SIMPLY PAPER

50 CREATIVE IDEAS FOR IMPROVING YOUR HOME

LINDA BARKER
PHOTOGRAPHY BY LIZZIE ORME

SIMPLY

PAPER

50 CREATIVE IDEAS FOR IMPROVING YOUR HOME

LINDA BARKER
PHOTOGRAPHY BY LIZZIE ORME

ANAYA PUBLISHERS LTD
LONDON

For Bob and Dot

First published in Great Britain in 1994 by

Anaya Publishers Ltd
Strode House, 44-50 Osnaburgh Street, London NW1 3ND

Series Editor	Janet Donin
Design	Watermark Communications Group Ltd
Photographer	Lizzie Orme
Assisted by	Sussie Bell
Stylist	Linda Barker
Jacket Design	Watermark Communications Group Ltd

British Library Cataloguing in Publication Data
Barker, Linda
Simply Paper: 50 Creative Ideas for Improving Your Home
1. Title 11. Orme, Lizzie
747.3

ISBN 1-85470-113-4
Typeset in Great Britain by
Watermark Communications Group Ltd
Colour reproduction by Scantrans Pte, Singapore
Printed and bound in Malaysia by Times Offset Ltd

Contents

Introduction
7

INTRODUCTION

Sitting on the bookcase in my living room is a bright blue aardvark. It's made of papier-mâché and is the source of endless enjoyment to my small daughter. I made it a few years ago now, about the same time that I pasted a pretty paper pergola to the wall in my hallway. Cut from ordinary wallpaper and intertwined with flowers it always cheers me up whenever I walk by. It was from projects like these that the idea for SIMPLY PAPER was inspired. If, until now, you thought that decorating with paper meant hanging the odd roll of textured wallpaper - think again!. For all my paper projects you will be working with newsprint, inexpensive wrapping papers or papers that were simply destined for the wastepaper bin. Yet within these pages I hope you will quickly discover that paper is not only extremely versatile and tremendous fun to use, but also a comparatively quick way to achieve startling and very rewarding results. Here I will show you how gloriously simple it is to create a stunning wallpaper effect in your kitchen by using nothing more exotic than a handful of photocopies. Hard to believe? Just wait and see! You'll be surprised at how these inexpensive materials can transform a boring kitchen into a room that looks as if it belongs in the pages of a design magazine - and it's such fun to achieve! Here too you'll find step-by-step instructions on copying my trellis pergola and, for a country dining room or kid's room, why not copy my colourful patchwork border? All these ideas are designed to encourage you to be more original in your approach to using paper, because I believe no one has to be limited to the obvious choice of patterned wallpaper versus textured wallpaper ever again. If you fancy sky blue tissue paper battlements and a paisley wrapping paper portcullis ... go wild! Experiment with all the different ideas that fill your imagination - after all, the main advantage of working with something as cheap as paper is that the worst mistake you can make is simply wasting a little time!

Decorating my home gives me so much pleasure that I hope I can encourage you to reap the rewards of working with paper too. But be sure to choose your papers carefully. I'd be the first to warn you that the price tags on some wallpapers will have you running out of the shop faster than you can say "pasting table"! They may look gorgeous but hardly ideal for fun and experimentation, which is why many of the projects in SIMPLY PAPER are based on the humble roll of lining paper or everyday newspapers. The delights of selecting and working with paper are all yours to explore and discover. If you want to stick real flowers under a photocopier and use the results as the basis for a grandiose design scheme, then go right ahead. As far as I'm concerned there's only one rule when decorating - if at the end of the job you really like the effect you've created, then you're doing it right!

Elsewhere in SIMPLY PAPER there are ideas for decorating plain cupboards, headboards and firescreens with ordinary wrapping papers and tricks with storage containers and jar labels. Although simple ideas like these don't cost a fortune to buy new, the point is you would never be able to buy anything so appealing, so creative and yet so obviously a bit of you. And I always think it's more fun to have something original than to settle for the mass-produced alternative. Just take a look at my fanciful vase or crown corona, fit for a princess. You can buy commercial examples quite easily but they're not half as much fun or original.

I've spent many years happily experimenting with all manner of techniques and results using wallpaper and I'm sure I've only scratched the surface of ideas when it comes to the world of paper. So why don't you start experimenting and having some fun too? I guarantee it won't be long before the last thing you'd ever think of doing with your paper is reading it!

Equipment

All you really need to copy any of the projects in this book are the everyday pieces of equipment you'll have in the humblest of tool boxes or the tiniest of kitchens. However if you are keen on do-it-yourself or an enthusiastic cook and you get hooked on these projects, it may be to your advantage to put everything back in the box or cupboard and make the small investment in new equipment.

PULPING

Some of the projects in Chapter One are based on paper pulp - see the step-by-step instructions - which I managed to produce quite easily in my small kitchen. However you will need a couple of large pieces of equipment if you're working in bulk. A **large bucket** or **plastic dustbin** is ideal for soaking the paper. This needs to be done in plenty of water to soften the fibres. A **large pan** for boiling the pulp is also essential. I use a large jam-making pan which I picked up at a secondhand shop, but any large, heavy bottomed pan will do, with or without a lid. A **large wooden spoon** is also useful to stir the paper as it boils in the pan. Make sure it has a long handle to avoid any scalds from the boiling pulp. A **mesh sieve or strainer** is needed to drain the water from the pulp, but since these are invariably quite small you may consider the old jam-making procedure of straining the pulp though muslin. A **whisk or blender** should be used to blend and break down the pulp. I have an electric hand blender which is ideal, but it is possible to use a manual whisk or even a balloon whisk, although it obviously takes much longer to achieve the same satisfactory results.
Basic tools like a **sturdy craft knife, good scissors, brushes** and a **set square** or **ruler** are probably readily available but may be worth an overhaul as they are used consistently for most of the projects.
Large plastic dust sheets and bags are not essential but I find them invaluable for protecting the work surfaces and floor when preparing the pulp. Plenty of cling film and plastic bags are also useful for storing the pulp, and for covering paint bushes and paste between projects.

Materials

PAPERS

To make pulp you can use any paper lying around your home. Of course different papers will produce different results and effects.

Newspapers are quite acceptable for making pulp but the newsprint does have a tendency to blacken the end result. I prefer to use newspaper for the layering technique, which is another form of papier-mâché. For layering rip the newspaper into small strips about 2.5cm/1in square and tear rather than cut the paper for the best effects.

Lining paper left over from decorating jobs or bought cheaply by the roll is an alternative to newspaper. It too should be torn into small strips for layering or use it to make good, clean pulp.

Paper pulp alternatives include paper towels, egg cartons, computer printout paper and tissue paper. The latter makes a very fine pulp which is ideal for intricate moulded details or for a fine, smooth finish.

Handmade papers are available in lots of different colours, textures and designs. You can buy these specifically for a particular project but I find it useful to have a supply on hand to use as an embellishment for papier-mâché objects. Some of the more expensive papers have delicate flower petals and leaves pressed into them, which form an integral part of the design and create an effect that's quite exquisite.

Sugar paper, at the other end of the scale, is not expensive and may be dyed to bright colours.

Wrapping papers seem to change with the seasons, so I buy one or two sheets whenever I see them until I have a good selection to choose from. Try to avoid shiny foil papers as these are difficult to stick onto paper. Wrapping papers can be used for overall decoration and also to cut up for individual motifs to use for découpage.

Wallpapers should only be bought if the design catches your eye, such as my trellis paper for the pergola, or if the design looks particularly useful to cut up for découpage.

Motifs are often available in sheet form featuring traditional images. These are useful to have as part of your découpage paper collection.

Source material images in black and white have been used throughout the book especially in the photocopied projects. You can find these in the Pictorial Archive series of books which are free from the copyright laws, which are used to protect original artwork.

Seed catalogues and magazines are very useful for compiling useful pictures for découpage and applied decoration. To keep papers neat and, perhaps more importantly, to protect them, roll them into a wide cardboard tube. A short length of plastic drainpipe works equally well.

TAPES
Brown gummed paper strips are very useful to join together pieces of card which form the support or structure of any object.

Masking tape can be used to hold card sections together while the glue or pulp dries.

PASTE
Cellulose wallpaper paste is used in the pulp-making process and for layering paper, as well as for the more conventional use of hanging wallpaper. Mix small quantities as you need them and save any left-overs in a small screw-topped jam jar to keep for further use.

White glue or PVA (polyvinyl acetate) is stronger than paper paste and is used in the pulp-making process to bind the pulp together. It is extremely useful and will store indefinitely if kept sealed. It can be thinned with water, or alternatively used as a sealant.

CARD AND CARDBOARD
I use corrugated cardboard to make the structures and supports for most of the projects in this book. Occasionally I have used thinner card, which can be easily bought or recycled from cereal packets.

PAINTS AND GESSO
Emulsion paint is used as a finishing layer on most paper objects before decoration. Sometimes I

substituted this with gesso which dries quickly and gives a thicker, tougher finish. It can also be sanded down to a smooth finish. Authentic gesso is tricky to prepare if you are not used to the process, so I suggest you use a commercial gesso powder, available in most good art and craft shops and easily prepared with water. Gesso also has the added advantage of softening the appearance of colours when they are applied over it, which also gives an aged quality.

Acrylic and gouache paints can be used for smaller objects such as the spice boxes.

SANDPAPER
Keep a supply of heavy, medium and fine gauge papers for sanding down gessoed objects or for preparing surfaces prior to decoration.

VARNISH
Varnish is important to seal and protect paper projects, which are vulnerable to normal wear and tear and can quickly become damaged. Varnish comes in two basic categories - water-based and oil-based. Both dry to a waterproof finish but I think better protection is achieved, on paper products, using the oil-based, polyurethane varnish. This is available in tins and applied with a brush, or in spray cans which are particularly useful when the object to be coated is quite small and requires several coats. I often recommend using three or four coats of varnish as this will greatly improve the appearance of an object.

FILLER
This is used in the paper pulp-making process, providing bulk to the paper mass and soaking up excess moisture.

LINSEED OIL
This is an important ingredient in the pulp-making process as it makes the pulp easier to handle. It also prevents the formation of mould and makes the dried pulp waterproof.

OIL OF CLOVES
This more unusual addition into the pulp actually encourages the longevity of the pulp and prevents it from "going off" before you have used it or before it has had chance to dry. It is sold in tiny bottles from health stores or pharmacists.

WIRE
Chicken wire can be bent and twisted to form various shapes onto which paper pulp can be applied. I use the finest weight of wire as this is easier to twist into shape and is perfectly adequate for the scale of objects in this book. It can be purchased as a length or on a roll.

FLORIST'S WIRE
Various thicknesses of florist's wire are always a part of my tool kit. It is useful for joining together sections of chicken wire or for strengthening weak joints. I even use it to thread long beads together as for the beaded curtain edging.

CHAPTER 1

PAPIER-MÂCHÉ

In this chapter you can really have fun, whether you are boiling pulp in a big pan or pasting on paper layers reminiscent of childhood hobbies. However, papier-mâché has come a long way since I made piggy banks from balloons and newspapers. Now the recipe for paper pulp results in a wonderful clay-like substance which can be sculpted, and even sanded, to produce smoother finishes. Layering paper can also produce surprising results, particularly when combined with collage techniques - just take a look at my star-shaped candlestick. And papier-mâché decorative projects couldn't be less expensive, all you basically need is the pulp paper and some cardboard - materials that were probably on their way to the wastepaper bin! So take a look at these simple yet attractive ideas - you could find just the inspiration you're looking for.

Paper Pulp

Paper pulp is simply made from newspaper. It is extremely versatile and, like clay, can be easily moulded.

MATERIALS

newspaper or lining paper

bucket

large pan

whisk or blender

sieve

2 Tbsp filler

2 Tbsp PVA glue

1 Tbsp linseed oil

few drops oil of cloves

2 Tbsp wallpaper paste

wooden spoon

Hints

Pulp projects take a long time to dry, so to speed up the process leave in a warm place (an airing cupboard) overnight or wait until the pulp has turned a much lighter shade indicating that it is dry.

1 Take four double-page sheets of newspaper, or a 2m/6ft length of lining paper. Tear into small pieces approx. 2.5cm/1in square. Place into a bucket and cover with cold water to soak overnight.

2 Transfer to a large pan, cover with water and boil for 20/30 mins. Mash into a pulp with a whisk or hand blender. Place in a sieve to strain out the water. Leave to cool. Squeeze out any excess water from the soft dough-like mass. Add the remaining ingredients and stir.

Sunflower Tiebacks

These tiebacks are particularly attractive when used with light-weight muslin or sheer curtains.

MATERIALS

pair of tiebacks

paper pulp

lightweight card

pencil

scissors

rubber gloves

yellow spray paint

knife

dark brown and dark green gouache

artist's brush

spray varnish

Hints

Use old tiebacks as a mould for the paper pulp. If their surface is heavily varnished or smooth, scratch with a small knife to give a suitable surface on which to stick the pulp.

1 Cover the front of the tieback with paper pulp and press firmly onto the surface. The pulp should be at least 2cm/3/4in thick. Using lightweight card, draw, then cut out 10x1cm/4x3/8in pointed petal shapes. Stick these into the sides of the pulp in two layers.

2 Having formed a complete sunflower, repeat the procedure for the second tieback. When thoroughly dry, protect your hands with rubber gloves and spray the flower with yellow paint on both front and back surfaces. Allow to dry.

3 Using the back of a knife, carefully curl each petal upwards, to form a natural flower shape. Paint the centre of the flower with the two shades of gouache, allowing some yellow to show through. Protect with three coats of varnish. Secure the tiebacks to the wall.

Star Motif Bowl

This attractive bowl is ideal for displaying pot pourri, fruit or dried flower heads.

MATERIALS

shallow bowl

cling film

paper pulp

large spoon

gesso powder

small dish

household paint brush

scissors

gold paper

emulsion paint

Hints

A shallow bowl is the easiest shape on which to mould paper pulp. When you become more experienced, experiment with a variety of different shapes.

1 Line the inside of your bowl with cling film. This acts as a releasing agent enabling you to remove the dried pulp easily. Coat the inside of the bowl with pulp using the back of a spoon to press it evenly into the curves. Maintain a thickness of 1.2cm/1/2in. Remove when dry. Press a thin sausage shaped piece of pulp to the base to form a support, leave to dry.

2 Mix the gesso powder in a dish, according to the manufacturer's instructions. Paint over the inside and outside surfaces of the bowl. The gesso will even out lumps and bumps creating a smoother finish. Additional coats of gesso will result in a more professional finish.

3 Cut the gold paper into star shapes and apply to the bowl while the gesso is still wet. You will find that they will stick quite easily to the surface. Don't worry if some gesso seeps over the stars, I think this adds character. Paint with emulsion.

Bed Corona

Any shape can be sculpted around
a basic half circle but this
charming crown would be ideal
for a little girl's bedroom. Secure
the corona to the wall with
L-shaped angle brackets.

MATERIALS

MDF (medium density fibreboard)

saw

tape measure

ruler

felt tip pen

cardboard

craft knife

staple gun/glue

paper strips

wallpaper paste

scissors

coloured paper

star wrapping paper

PVA glue

screw hooks

L-shaped brackets

Hints

The mosaic squares can be cut from any
paper - coloured sweet wrappers would
create a jewelled look.

1 Cut a semi-circle of MDF approx 60cm/2ft diameter. Use a ruler to draw the pointed crown shape on card to this width. Each point should have a base measurement of approx 30cm/12in. Create half points on the outer edges. Using a craft knife cut out the crown shape.

2 Staple or glue the base of the crown to the edge of the MDF so the points face downwards. Stick torn strips of paper over the shape with wallpaper paste. Allow the first layer to dry before applying the next layer in the opposite direction. Apply at least five layers.

3 Cut tiny squares of coloured paper and glue to the crown with wallpaper paste in a mosaic fashion. Cut stars from wrapping paper and glue at random over the crown to complete the look. Screw hooks, 7.5cm/3in apart, under the rim of the corona to hold the curtain.

Seashore Blind Edging

Capturing the memories of
summer holidays, this edging
is perfect for a child's room
or bathroom.

MATERIALS

pencil

cardboard

scissors

paper pulp

white emulsion

bowl

artist's paint brush

artist's acrylic paints

gloss varnish

needle

strong thread

blind

Hints

You could use a child's drawings as
inspiration for these sea creatures or get
your children to draw their own shapes
on cardboard.

1 Draw elementary fish shapes onto a piece of cardboard. Include a simple starfish and a three pronged outline to resemble seaweed. Cut out the shapes and sandwich between two layers of paper pulp. The finished shape should be at least 1.2cm/1/2in thick.

2 Allow the shapes to dry. Pour a little white emulsion paint into a bowl and paint both sides of the shapes. Apply enough layers of paint to achieve the surface you want. Let each coat dry before applying the next to achieve a smooth finish.

3 Use acrylic paints to colour the fish and seaweed. Refer to children's story books, if necessary, for colour and detail ideas. When dry apply gloss varnish to protect. Use a darning needle to pierce each shape, then sew to the blind hem with strong thread.

Sunburst Mirror

Truly fanciful, this mirror will add a decorative touch to any wall. The shape also makes an imaginative picture frame.

MATERIALS

pencil

corrugated cardboard

paper pulp

gesso powder

bowl

household paint brush

sandpaper

metallic paint

gloss varnish

strong adhesive

small mirror

plate hooks

Hints

Use plate hooks attached to the back of the mirror to hang it on the wall.

1 Decide on the overall size of the mirror. Draw a circle to this dimension on the corrugated cardboard, with a smaller circle, at least 15cm/6in diameter, in the centre. Outline the eight points of your sun burst shape between the two circles. Apply the paper pulp within the shape leaving central circle uncovered.

2 Remove the paper pulp shape from the cardboard when dry. Mix the gesso powder in a bowl and paint two layers over the front and back surfaces of the sun shape. Allow the first coat to dry before applying the second and sand down between coats for a smoother finish.

3 Paint the sun shape with a water-based metallic paint. The surface will be slightly uneven, so push the paint into the small lumps and bumps until it is completely covered. Protect the finished mirror frame with two layers of gloss varnish. Use a strong adhesive to stick the mirror to the back of the frame.

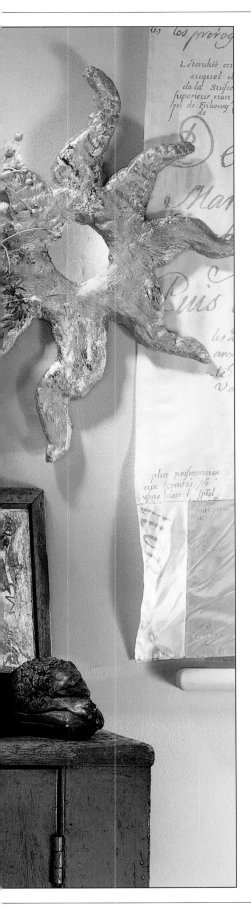

Decorative Bowl

I love the bizarre shape of this bowl, which will make an eye-catching centrepiece for any table.

MATERIALS

tin snips	paper pulp
chicken wire	emulsion paint
protective gloves	household paint brush
pliers	gilt wax
florist's wire	matt varnish

Hints

Chicken wire can be quite difficult to mould so always wear protective gloves.

1 Cut chicken wire into a 35.5x51cm/ 14x20in rectangle and two 5x30cm/2x12in pieces. Wearing gloves and using pliers, twist the rectangle into a tube shape. Squeeze wire together about 20cm/8in from one end, then sculpt the bowl and stand. Create the decorative shapes from the narrow wire pieces.

2 Cut 15cm/6in lengths of florist's wire and use to join the decorative pieces to the bowl. Push one end of the wire through the decorative piece, then through the bowl. Twist to hold together, then snip off excess wire with pliers. Repeat at each end.

3 Apply the paper pulp to the bowl in small amounts until it is completely covered both inside and out. Stand the bowl upright and smooth out the pulp to a thickness of 1.2cm/1/2in. Roll a small ball of pulp and position on top of one twisted side decoration.

4 When the pulp is dry, apply coloured emulsion paint to the inside and outside of the bowl and one side decoration. Use the gilt wax to colour the remaining side decoration. Apply with your fingers, rubbing well into the textured surface. Finish with a coat of matt varnish.

Star Candlestick

Some wrapping papers are just too good to throw away after use, so I have chosen one of my favourites to decorate this candlestick.

MATERIALS

corrugated cardboard

pencil

ruler

scissors

craft knife

masking tape

paper for layering

wallpaper paste

wrapping paper

gloss varnish

Hints

If you find it impossible to draw a star freehand, use a star-shaped biscuit cutter for your outline.

1 Draw a five-pointed star within a 10cm/4in diameter circle on the cardboard. Cut out three star shapes. Cut a 2.5cm/1in diameter circle in the centre of one star. Make a tube from an 18x7.5cm/7x3in piece of cardboard. Cut 2.5cm/1in from one end and push into the centre of the cut star.

2 Use masking tape to secure and cover the base of this star - this is the candlestick top. Join the remaining stars to one end of the tube with masking tape. Glue the candlestick top to the other end of the tube. Coat with five layers of paper using the wallpaper paste. Allow to dry thoroughly between layers.

3 Use patterned wrapping paper to decorate the candlestick. Tear some paper pieces and cut others for a more interesting appearance. Apply to the candlestick with wallpaper paste. Allow to dry thoroughly then protect with a coat of varnish.

Napkin Rings

Choose a decorative border with more than one element to its design for this decorative effect.

MATERIALS

ruler	green paper
pencil	printed paper border
corrugated cardboard	green card
scissors	craft knife
gummed paper strip	strong glue
paper for layering	spray-on varnish
wallpaper paste	

Hints

Use a bottle to support the napkin ring while coating the outside with varnish. When dry varnish the inside of the ring.

1 Using a ruler and pencil, draw two 18x5cm/7x2in rectangles on corrugated cardboard. Cut out each rectangle and twist into a ring. Secure the join with a gummed paper strip. Tear the paper into strips ready for layering.

2 Apply paper strips to each ring with wallpaper paste. Alternate the direction of each layer until you have built up five layers. Allow to dry between each layer. Glue small strips of green paper to the inside of each napkin ring to line. Don't worry if the dye seeps through.

3 Choose a paper border with a definite design like mine. I cut the checked edge from my paper border and used wallpaper paste to stick it in bands around the outside of each napkin ring. The vegetable prints were then glued to a piece of green card before cutting out with a craft knife.

4 Use strong glue to stick the vegetable prints securely to the front of each napkin ring. Wait until this is completely dry before coating inside and out with a layer of varnish. The varnish will also considerably strengthen the ring.

Storage Jar Lids

I thought these terracotta pots were too attractive to use in the garden so I made paper lids and turned them into useful, yet inexpensive, storage jars.

MATERIALS

terracotta pots

pencil

cardboard

scissors

paper pulp

four colours of handmade papers

wallpaper paste

varnish

Hints

The pulp will dry evenly if you place the lids on a wire cooling rack allowing the air to circulate freely.

1 Using the top of a terracotta pot as a guide, draw a circle on a piece of cardboard for each lid. Enlarge the circle by approx 1.2cm/1/2in and cut on this line to make a lid slightly larger than your pot.

2 Cover the lid on both sides with paper pulp approx 1.2cm/1/2in thick. Create a variety of shapes with the pulp - flat disks, ovals and round beads - and layer onto the centre top of each lid. Roll more pulp into a thin sausage shape and press onto the underside of the lid to form a lip.

3 Leave the pulp lids to dry thoroughly until they are hard to the touch. Tear the handmade paper into 1.2cm/1/2in strips and, using a little wallpaper paste, apply to the lids in a random fashion. I have used a different colour paper for each layer of pulp. Varnish to protect.

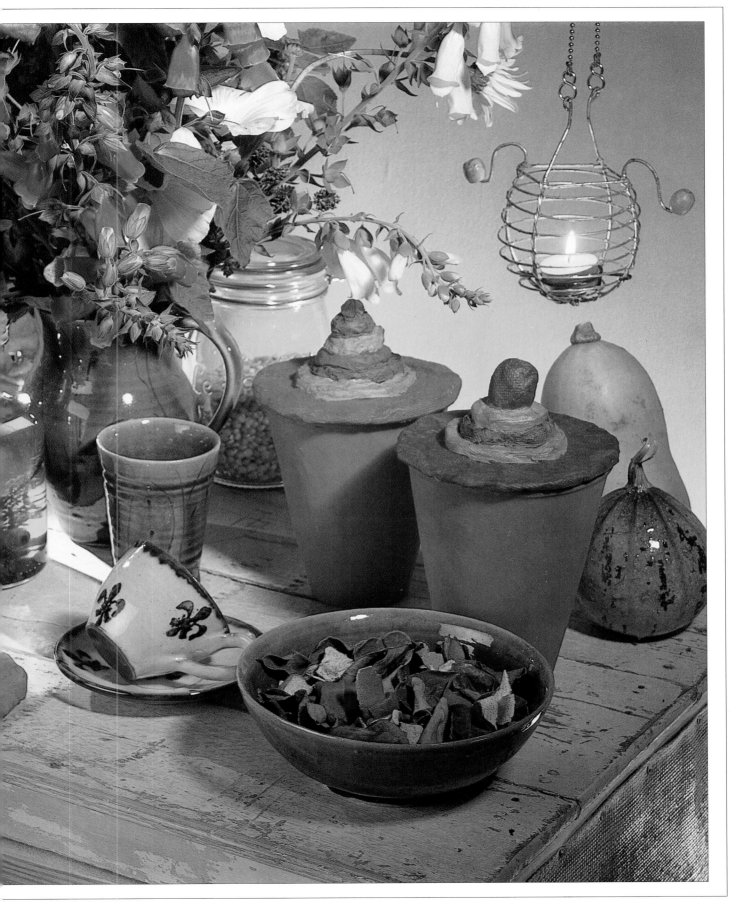

Letter Rack

If you keep losing bills and forgetting to write letters, this decorative rack is the ideal organiser.

MATERIALS

cardboard	paper for layering
pencil	wallpaper paste
dinner plate	wrapping paper
tea plate	heart motif
saucer	string
scissors	sealing wax
ruler	coin
gummed paper strip	plasticine

Hints

I used a wrapping paper printed with stamps and postmarks but if you can't find anything similar use a collage of old letters and real stamps instead.

1 On a piece of cardboard draw the outlines of a dinner plate, tea plate and saucer. Cut around the curved edges and across the centre and sides for each section. You will see that each diminishes in size. Cut a cardboard base to the length of the dinner plate's diameter and 12.5cm/5in wide.

2 Use gummed paper strips to assemble the letter rack as shown. Paste torn paper pieces over the entire cardboard surface. Build up at least five layers. Alternate the direction of each layer and allow each to dry before applying the next.

3 Tear the printed wrapping paper into varying sized pieces and, using the wallpaper paste to apply, cover the letter rack. Build up an interesting collage effect. Some pieces may also be cut as a contrast to the torn edges.

4 For the final decorative touch glue cut-out hearts at random over the surface, then bind the rack with string for a packaged look. Apply sealing wax to the string joins then stick a coin into the plasticine and use to press firmly into the soft wax leaving a distinctive impression.

Arrow-shaped Finials

These stunning arrow-shaped finials will bring a touch of grandeur to your curtains and windows.

MATERIALS

tin snips

chicken wire

curtain pole

paper pulp

varnish

gesso powder

bowl

household paint brush

emulsion paints

artist's paint brush

Hints

Experiment with different shaped finials like fanciful coils and fleur-de-lis.

1 Use the tin snips to cut two 30cm/12in squares of chicken wire. To form the cylindrical base sections make two 10cm/4in cuts, each 10cm/4in in from the outside edges of the base. Twist these cut sections around to fit the pole. Bend the remaining wire to form the arrowhead and feather.

2 Cover the wire shapes with paper pulp, pressing it firmly into the chicken wire on all sides. Make sure that the centres of the cylindrical shapes are free of pulp. Finish by smoothing the pulp with your hands until the surface is even. Leave to dry.

3 Mix the gesso powder with water in a small bowl, according to the manufacturer's instructions. Use an old paint brush to apply liberally to the surfaces of the arrow. Allow one side to dry before coating the other. The gesso will help to even out the surface ready for painting.

Beaded Curtain Edging

These long beads with their tasselled ends look very elegant and will give weight to the hem of a lightweight fabric curtain.

MATERIALS

scraps of wallpaper

scissors

wallpaper paste

florist's wire

coloured handmade paper

varnish

brush

gold thread

beads

needle

Hints

Use beads from an old necklace to decorate the ends of the paper beads.

1 Cut the wallpaper into 12.5x10cm/5 x4in rectangles. Shape to a point on one long side so the paper will roll easily. Apply paste to the wallpaper and, starting at the point, roll around a length of florist's wire to form the long bead shape. The wire maintains a hole through the centre of the bead.

2 Remove the wire and paste small, torn pieces of the handmade paper over the bead until it is covered. One layer of paper should be sufficient. Be careful not to paste any paper over the holes at either end. When dry, varnish to protect.

3 Pass gold thread through the paper bead using a piece of wire that's looped to resemble a long needle. Add several real beads to the end. Finish with a tassel made from eight loops of thread cut at one end and bound with more thread at the other. Sew completed beads to the curtain hem.

4 Use emulsion paint to colour the arrow finials. I have used two similar colours to create a mottled pattern. When this is dry, use the darker colour to paint in the details of the arrow tail feathers. Apply one quick brush stroke for each mark. Varnish.

CHAPTER 2

PHOTOCOPIES

What a wonderful invention - the photocopier! Who would believe that the most intricate and elaborate projects in this chapter have all been made possible by the simple touch of a button? Well, okay, you need an element of imagination to get the ideas started, but hopefully I will be able to provide you with more than enough and then the rest is up to you! There are simple projects here to transform virtually any room in the house, from an alternative to kitchen wallpaper to a remarkable bathroom cabinet. All have to be seen to be believed, but I guarantee a visit to the bathroom or kitchen will never be quite so much fun. And I'm willing to bet you've never seen such a fabulous shade of blue as my photocopied cornflower. So don't be fazed by the technology, it's there for us to use and explore!

Spice Storage Boxes

These unique little containers soon replaced the conventional glass storage jars in my kitchen.

MATERIALS

watercolours
artist's brush
small wooden boxes
sandpaper
photocopied pictures
pinking scissors
PVA glue
crepe paper
darning needle
string
brass eyelets
raffia
paper ribbon

Hints

I colour-photocopied small herb pictures from a gardening book to decorate the front of these boxes.

1 Using the watercolours, paint a thin layer of colour over all four sides of the boxes. When dry, lightly rub the surface with sandpaper to remove some of the printed lettering and a little watercolour paint. This creates a pleasant, weathered finish to the box.

2 Choose a picture to represent the contents of each storage box and make a colour photocopy. Use the reducing and enlarging facility on the machine to achieve the right image size for your box. Cut the edges with pinking scissors and glue onto the front of the box.

3 Make a bag from crepe paper. The base should be slightly larger than the box base. The width of each side is equal to two sides of the box and the height is two and a half times that of the box. Thread a darning needle with fine string and sew the bag together. Cut the top with pinking scissors.

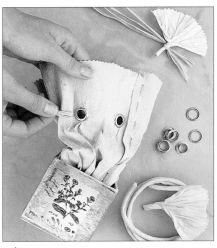

4 Position the eyelets approx 10cm/4in from the top edge of the crepe paper bag and thread through with raffia. Tie a 5cm/2in piece of paper ribbon to each end of the raffia and tease open to create a pretty fan. Put a bag inside each storage box.

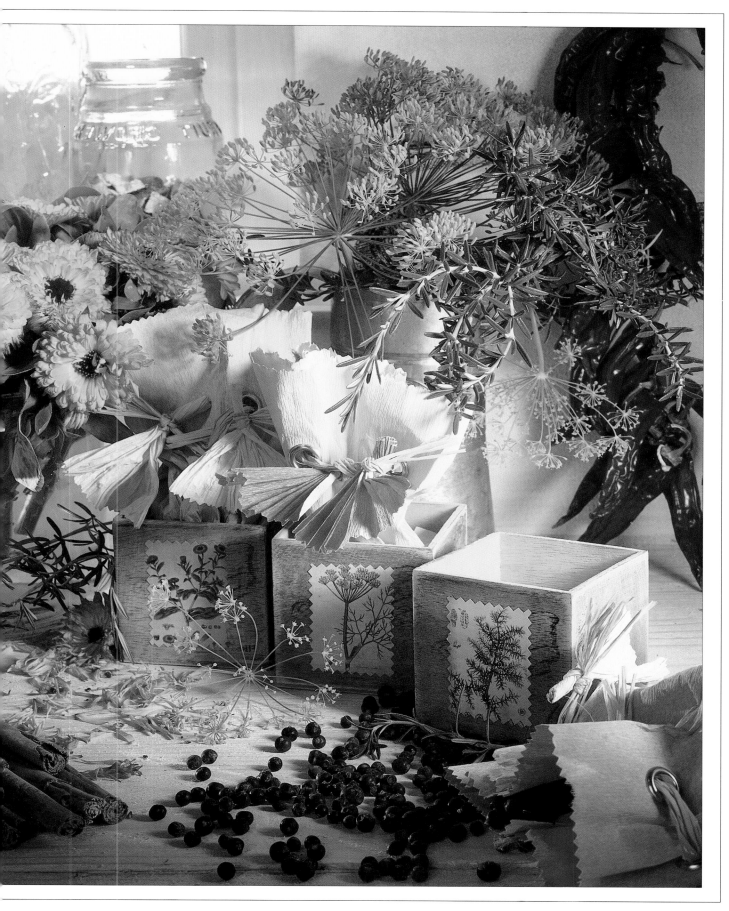

Cafe Mug Rack

Mug racks are so useful but are often very plain so I decided to make a feature of this one and pattern it with a photocopied sign.

MATERIALS

piece of wood

photocopied image

PVA glue

household paint brush

emulsion paint (terracotta and white)

wire wool

sandpaper

watercolours

artist's paint brush

brass hooks

Hints

Find a cafe or menu sign which would look fun in a kitchen and enlarge the image on a photocopier to fit the wooden rack.

1 Select a piece of wood for your rack measuring approx. 38x15cm/15x6in and at least 2.5cm/1in thick to hold the hooks. Use these dimensions to make the photocopy enlargement. Glue the photocopy to the wood with PVA glue.

2 Use a dry brush to paint an uneven layer of terracotta emulsion paint over the front surface of the wood. Allow the black and white image of the photocopy to show through. When dry remove a little paint by rubbing the surface carefully with wire wool and sandpaper.

3 Use black watercolour to paint over some of the lettering to give it an individual hand-painted quality. Use other colours to paint in further details shown on your image. I used green paint to define the leaf pattern on my design.

4 Use the white emulsion paint to highlight some of the lettering and contrast with the previously applied black paint. Dilute the paint with 50% water and paint broad, mottled patches over the sign to give it an aged and faded appearance. Mount the brass hooks.

Tea Tray

Images of tea cups, pots and jugs were the perfect decoration for this tray. Remember if you are photocopying from a source book be sure to use one that has a free copyright.

MATERIALS

photocopied designs

scissors

tray

craft knife

watercolours

artist's paint brush

spray paint

sandpaper

PVA glue

gloss varnish

Hints

If you can't be bothered to paint lots of little images, choose just one large central motif.

1 Photocopying can be expensive so select a page from a copyright-free booklet with the most illustrations to choose from. Randomly cut out a variety of the images until you have enough to cover your tray completely in a pleasing design.

2 Carefully cut around each image again, this time using a craft knife to get as close to the printed edge as you can. Use watercolours to paint each image. The black and white gradations on the photocopy will help you to define and highlight the shading in the right areas.

3 I used a pale pink spray paint to colour my tray. When this was dry I carefully rubbed off some pink paint with sandpaper. This revealed a little of the original green colour beneath to simulate aging. Glue the images to the tray. When dry protect the surface with three layers of varnish.

Storage Jar Labels

If you like to show off your home-made produce it can be infuriating not to have attractive labels. So why compromise? Copy my eye-catching designs instead.

MATERIALS

photocopied letters

scissors

two or three scraps of handmade papers

PVA glue

black and white photocopied pictures

watercolours

artist's paint brush

sterilised jar

home-made produce

·decorative string

Hints

You can adapt this idea to make labels for any containers or storage boxes, even name plates for your children's rooms.

1 Photocopy the decorative letters and cut out an interesting mix of shapes to make up the label name. Tear a rectangle from a piece of handmade paper on which to position all the letters. Tear two smaller scraps of paper to glue onto the first piece to make the label more interesting.

2 Select a relevant print to illustrate the produce and photocopy. Use the watercolours to tint this image, allowing the printed detail to show through. Assemble all the pieces to make up the label and glue in position on the rectangular piece of paper.

3 Use PVA glue to stick the whole label onto the sterilised jar ensuring that all the edges are firmly stuck. Fill the jar with the produce and use two pieces of paper to make a date label for the goods. Tie this to the neck of the jar with decorative string.

Biscuit Barrel

This is a fascinating way of using a colour photocopier and gives an attractive finish to a simple container.

MATERIALS

scissors

handmade paper

wooden storage container

real flowers

photocopied print

PVA glue

emulsion paint

household paint brush

spray varnish

Hints

You could place any flower on the photocopier but choose one with an intense colour such as this cornflower.

1 Cut a piece of handmade paper to cover one side of the barrel. Mine has eight sides but yours may have more or less, it doesn't matter. Place your chosen flower in the centre of the paper. Colour photocopy this as many times as you have sides on your box.

2 Cut around the copied print and glue the image onto the container using the PVA glue. Smooth out any air bubbles that may appear under the surface. Continue applying the prints in this way until you have covered the container.

3 Paint the lid of the barrel an appropriate shade, using the emulsion paint. You will probably need two coats for good coverage. When completely dry, use a spray varnish to seal and protect the finished container.

Dado Border

This is an inexpensive way of creating a unique look for any room. I have used a sophisticated border for a living room, but you could copy a child's drawing to create a personal border for a bedroom.

MATERIALS

tape measure

image to be copied

sponge

water

gummed paper strip

wooden board

sepia watercolour paint

artist's paint brush

craft knife

wallpaper paste

Hints

If you prefer, use the border at picture rail height or to define a small window or doorway.

1 Measure the width of the walls where you want to use the border. Measure the length of your chosen image, then divide this figure into the width of your walls to give you the number of photocopies needed. Copy enough border pieces plus four or five extra.

2 To prevent the paper strips from wrinkling when pasted to the wall, pre-stretch them by applying a wet sponge to the front and back of each piece. Use the gummed paper strip to stick each to a wooden board. Don't worry if a little black dye comes out of the prints.

3 While the border strips are still damp, tint the surface with diluted watercolour. Leave the strips to dry overnight. Use a craft knife to remove them from the board, making sure the edges are quite square. Use wallpaper paste to position on your wall approx. 81.5cm/32in from the floor.

Print Room Screen

This type of cutting and pasting of prints was particularly popular in the seventeenth century. But the inspiration for my screen was borrowed from the many historical houses I have visited.

MATERIALS

photocopied prints	emulsion paint
photocopied borders	household brush
ruler	folding screen
set square	PVA glue diluted 50/50 with water
scissors	gloss varnish

Hints

Look for prints in secondhand shops or antique markets. Photocopies can be tinted with tea to simulate old age. My more elaborate borders come ready to cut out and are available by mail order from the National Trust (address on page 112).

1 Assemble the prints and borders together and use a ruler and set square to outline a variety of shapes to make a more interesting screen. It's surprising how much material you will need to cover the screen so be prepared! Cut out each design and shape ready for pasting.

2 Paint the screen with emulsion paint. Position the prints and borders on the screen. Be imaginative and don't always group the prints in a totally symmetrical way. Try framing a small print with a deep border for an original effect.

3 When you are happy with the grouping and arrangement of the prints start to glue them down. I find it easier to position and glue two sides of the border first, then glue the print in the middle, lining it up squarely to the corners. Finally glue the remaining edges of the borders.

4 If you think your screen needs more detail, look out for these wonderful printed ribbons, bows and lion heads. They are perfect for adding a theatrical touch to your screen. Cut out carefully and glue around the prints. Finish with at least two coats of gloss varnish.

Bathroom Cabinet

A simple glass-fronted cabinet can be transformed, with a few basic materials and a little imagination, to resemble the look of patterned glass.

MATERIALS

scissors

self-adhesive clear plastic

bathroom cabinet

coloured tissue paper

photocopied fish pictures

PVA glue

watercolours

artist's paint brush

Hints

If you can find only coloured pictures of fish, you can colour- photocopy them, but I think hand-tinted ones look more original.

1 Cut a piece of self-adhesive clear plastic to the same internal measurements as the glass panel in your cabinet door. Place the plastic, clear side facing down, on the front of the door panel, then peel off its backing paper, sticky side is uppermost.

2 Tear strips of coloured tissue paper and place these in vertical, overlapping lines, on the plastic to resemble seaweed. Arrange the "seaweed" strips to look decoratively pleasing with equal spaces between each line.

3 Select your fish pictures and photocopy them, enlarging or reducing their size to fit. Cut out carefully and stick over the tissue panels with PVA glue. Tint each fish with watercolours, allowing the print to show through. Remove the completed panel and stick to the inside of the glass door panel.

Decorated Drawers

I used pictures torn from an old diary for these drawers but if you want to use pictures from a book simply colour-photocopy the images instead.

MATERIALS

coloured pictures

craft knife

painted drawers

PVA glue

watercolour paint

white emulsion paint

household paint brush

wire wool

Hints

Instead of bird images you could choose pictures that represent the contents of the drawers - toys for a child's room, tools or sewing materials for practical use, even make-up or jewellery for the dressing table.

1 Assemble the pictures to be used. I collected as many bird images as I could to cover the front panels of these drawers. It's probably better to cut out more images than you think you will need so you can make a collage of the pieces.

2 Cut out the images neatly with the craft knife. Arrange on the drawer fronts until you are satisfied with the design. You may need to remove some or all of the drawer knobs. When you are satisfied with the design glue the pictures with PVA.

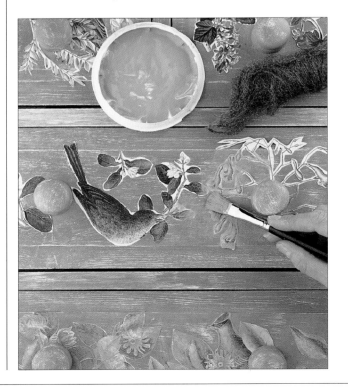

3 To make the cut images blend with the painted surface, mix a little watercolour with white emulsion until you have a colour close to that on the drawers. Paint this sparingly over the pictures. Rub away some of the wet paint with wire wool to add further detail.

Kitchen Cupboard Door Trellis

If you'd like a new look for your kitchen cupboards, simply transform your existing doors with this painted paper trellis.

MATERIALS

cartridge paper

pencil

craft knife

ruler

wallpaper

green emulsion paint

set square

household paint brush

PVA glue

photocopied flowers

varnish

Hints

If you have melamine doors paint them with eggshell paint, together with the relevant primer and undercoat. Wooden doors will need stripping with a hard surface remover before painting with emulsion paint.

1 Make a template for the trellis from cartridge paper cut to the size of the door panel. If there isn't a panel, make a paper one 5cm/2in narrower all round than the door. Cut wallpaper to cover each door panel and paint with green emulsion.

2 On the cartridge paper template draw a border line 2.5cm/1in from each side. Using the set square and starting in one corner at the border line draw diagonal lines across the panel, 2.5cm/1in apart. Repeat from the opposite corner to complete the trellis design.

3 Place cartridge paper panel over wallpaper panel. Cut out the squares between the trellis lines, through both panels. Allow 3mm/1/8in on each side of the drawn line before cutting. You now have a cartridge paper template and a wallpaper panel for the first door.

4 Place the flowers under a colour photocopier. I used a tiny flower to fit easily inside the small trellis diamonds. Cut out photocopied flowers and glue one flower inside a trellis diamond to form a regular pattern across the door. Varnish.

Kitchen Wall Decoration

I love the originality of using photocopies as a wall decoration in this kitchen and you won't believe how simple it is to create!

rustic animal prints

craft knife

A4 bond paper

household paint brush

wallpaper paste

PVA glue diluted 50/50 with water

cotton cloth

watercolours

paint brushes

Hints

This photocopied image can be used effectively as a border or frieze as well as an all-over pattern.

1 Select the images to be used. I have chosen rustic prints from one of the many copyright-free books. Cut out and paste each image to be used onto a sheet of plain paper. Photocopy this page to give you enough prints to cover your walls.

2 Cut out each print carefully, as close to the outline as you can. Use a paint brush and the diluted PVA glue to coat both sides of each print, then stick onto the wall. Smooth flat with a cotton cloth to remove any trapped air and excess glue.

3 If your kitchen walls are not white, the photocopied print may stand out too much, so colourwash the prints with a diluted solution of the kitchen wall paint until the outline blends in well. Use the watercolours to tint each print. Protect with the diluted PVA.

CHAPTER 3

DECORATIVE PAPERS

Lots of the projects in this chapter are made from materials that were destined to be thrown away - ends of wallpaper rolls, or the odd piece of paper ribbon that's not really long enough to be of much use. And if you are buying these materials, always look for a "recycled" label. In that way we can at least be conscious of our environment in what is actually a very wasteful, throw-away society. There are literally hundreds of ways to use paper decoratively around the home, often in the most unexpected ways. Paper ribbon doesn't always have to be used for tying extravagant bows on presents. Why not use it to tie a bundle of shells and pebbles and make yourself a wonderful curtain tieback? It's certainly unique!

Wastepaper Bin

This is designed as a cover for an ugly plastic waste bin. Simply slot it over your bin for a stylish way to dispose of rubbish.

MATERIALS

tape measure

coloured cardboard

pencil

ruler

stencil

craft knife

hole punch

coloured raffia

scissors

Hints

If you don't have a stencil you could simply draw around an object with an interesting outline.

1 Measure the sides and base of your wastepaper bin. Add 6mm/1/4in all round for an easier fit. Cut four sides and one base panel from the coloured cardboard to these dimensions. Position your stencil on the cardboard. My seahorse is centrally placed 5cm/2in below the top edge. Draw around the stencil outline.

2 Cut out the seahorse using a craft knife. Draw a line 2.5cm/1in in from the edges of the five panels (except for the top edge of each side panel). Mark points at 5cm/2in intervals along this line with a pencil. Use the hole punch to make holes at these points.

3 Cut the coloured raffia into 12.5cm/5in lengths. Position two side pieces side by side and thread the raffia through the top hole in each. Tie in a bow. Repeat for all the other holes. Assemble remaining sides and base panel in the same way until wastepaper bin cover is complete.

Pleated Lampshade

Good quality, attractive wrapping papers are so inexpensive you can make lampshades to complement any room in the home and change them as often as you please.

MATERIALS

lampshade frame

tape measure

wrapping paper

scissors

glue

coin

skewer

raffia

masking tape

Hints

Use a low-watt lightbulb for the lamp as anything higher may scorch the paper shade.

1 Measure the height of the frame and add 5cm/2in to give the depth of your shade. Measure the bottom ring of the frame and double this to give you the length of paper required. Cut out the paper, join strips with glue if necessary. Fold the paper concertina-style into 2.5cm/1in wide folds.

2 When completely folded, join the side edges together by tucking one fold inside another and securing with glue. If you have an obvious design on your paper try matching the pattern, even if you need to sacrifice the odd fold or two.

3 To cut the scalloped bottom edge, pinch together three or four folds and cut into a half circle. If you prefer, use a coin as a template while cutting. Punch holes through the centre of each fold, 2.5cm/1in from the top edge of the shade, using a skewer.

4 Thread raffia through the punched holes. Bind the ends with masking tape to make this easier. Pull the top of the shade together leaving an opening wide enough to fit over the frame. Tie the raffia. Put glue on the top and bottom rings of the frame to hold the shade in place.

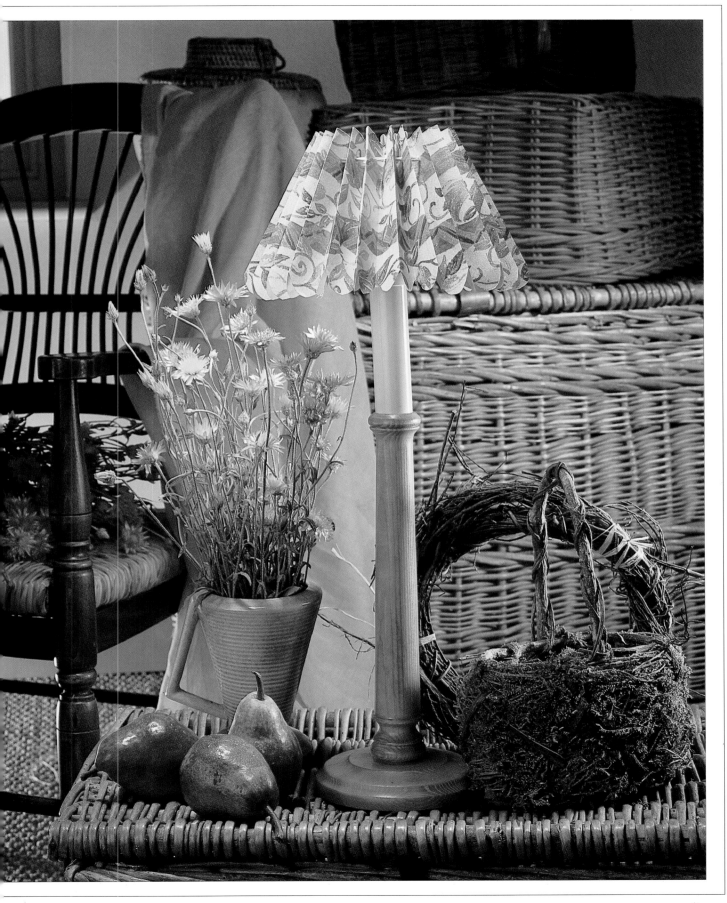

Shelf Ornamenta

These oak leaves form a wreath that will add a classical look to uninteresting shelves or bookcases.

MATERIALS

gold paper

glue

tracing paper

stiff cardboard

pen

craft knife

scissors

three corks

Hints

You could also use these leaves to decorate the edge of a mirror or picture frame.

1 Glue two sheets of gold paper together so that when you cut out the paper leaves they will look the same on the front and back. Trace our template on to cardboard and use to draw the leaves on the gold paper. Cut out using a craft knife.

2 On one side of each leaf score lines to resemble the natural veins in oak leaves. Use a pair of closed scissors and press down firmly enough to make a visible mark, but be careful not to tear the paper. Look at a real oak leaf for inspiration.

3 From the cardboard, cut a curved support stand, like ours. Don't worry if it is not perfectly symmetrical as the leaves will cover it completely. Glue the base of each leaf to the cardboard, carefully overlapping them to cover the stand. Glue three corks in a triangular arrangement on your shelf to support the stand.

Shell Decorated Book

This is a fanciful idea to use as a diary, note book or even photograph album.

MATERIALS

heavy cardboard

craft knife

masking tape

coloured paper for inside

ruler

pencil

hole punch

brown paper

PVA glue

skewer

wrapping paper

decorative string

drill and bit

shells

raffia

Hints

Chose a subtle wrapping paper for the book cover so the shell detail can be seen. Use several shades of paper for an attractive look inside.

1 Decide on the overall size of the book you wish to make and cut a front and back cover from the cardboard. Cut a spine to the height of the cover and 2.5cm/1in wide. Join the spine to the front and back covers with masking tape.

2 Cut the internal pages to size if they need trimming. Use a paper punch to make holes in the left-hand side of the pages and also through the front and back cover, having measured the position of the holes with a ruler and pencil beforehand.

3 Glue the wrapping paper to the cardboard book cover, joining any sheets as necessary. Cut away the excess paper, leaving a border of 7.5cm/3in around all edges. Cut a square from each corner of the border, then turn in and glue to the inside of the book.

4 Cut a piece of brown paper for the inside cover, large enough to conceal all the wrapping paper edges, glue down. Feel for the punched holes in the cover, then push a skewer through the brown paper at these points.

5 Thread the string through the punched holes of the back cover, then through the paper pages and finally through to the front book cover; knot the string to secure. Separate the strands of the string and knot each end. Drill a hole through each shell. Thread with raffia and tie to each strand of string.

Curtain Tiebacks

Any shells or attractive pebbles would look good decorating this tieback. I have even added corks and driftwood for a truly "beachcomber" look.

MATERIALS

paper ribbon in various colours

scissors

crepe paper

string

florist's wire

pliers

small terracotta plant pots

drill and bit

shells

corks

driftwood

pebbles

raffia

Hints

Twist a piece of wire to the centre of each string loop to make it easier to push this through the terracotta plant pots.

1 Cut at least four strips of paper ribbon into 1m/40in lengths and tease the crinkled paper out with your fingers. Cut similar lengths from the crepe paper. Additional lengths of ribbon and paper will make a wider tieback.

2 Cut three 145cm/57in lengths of string and plait together. Plait together all the paper and ribbon strips. Twist a piece of wire with the extra length of string and fold to form a loop. Push each loop through a plant pot.

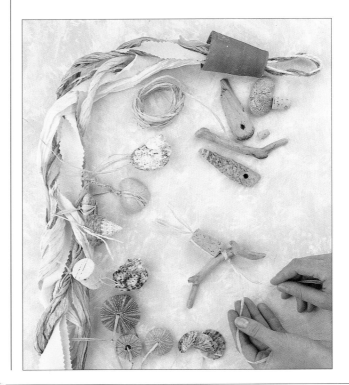

3 Drill small holes through all the shells, corks, wood and pebbles to be strung. Any difficult items can be held in a cradle of raffia, knotted on both sides of the item. Attach all the decorations to the tiebacks with raffia, making sure they will hang across the front of the curtain.

Star Wall Decoration

These stars can look magical in any room. Use against a mottled dark blue ceiling to create a celestial look.

MATERIALS

template paper

spray glue or sticky tape

yellow and orange stiff paper or thin cardboard

craft knife

glue

Hints

You could copy this idea in any coloured card and use for Christmas tree decorations.

1 Use a photocopier to enlarge our template to your preferred star size. For my stars the template has been enlarged by 100%, to double its size, but you could have smaller ones if you prefer. Use spray glue or tape to fix the photocopy to the cardboard and cut around this edge.

2 Fold the points of the stars following the fold lines on the template as a guide. Bend back the tabs. Glue the smaller shape to the larger one, along the tab edges. Press this into the main shape. Glue the stars to the wall along the tab edges.

Vase Decoration

This is a simple, yet decorative idea to give a unique look to an inexpensive vase or lampshade base.

MATERIALS

paper strips

paste

florist's wire

emulsion paints

household paint brush

strong adhesive

soft cloth

Hints

The paper strips are wired so they will coil easily. Experiment with longer pieces for more complicated coils.

1 Moisten each paper strip with a little paste and coil this around a length of florist's wire until it is completely covered. Make sure that the ends of the wire are also covered so the wire inside is not visible.

2 Use a little emulsion to paint each coil and twist it into the desired shape while the paint is still wet. Leave to dry and touch up the colour with a second coat if necessary. Use a paint colour to co-ordinate with the vase.

3 Stick the coils onto the vase using a strong adhesive. Leave the glue to dry and then brush a little darker shade of paint over the coils. Wipe a little off while it is still wet. You will find that some paint is held in the recesses for an unusual effect.

Trellis Pergola

This method of applying wallpaper is ideal for a small area like a hallway.

MATERIALS

trellis wallpaper

wallpaper paste

paste brush

scissors

dinner plate

craft knife

tape

Hints

If you can't find trellis patterned wallpaper, experiment with striped or checked paper instead.

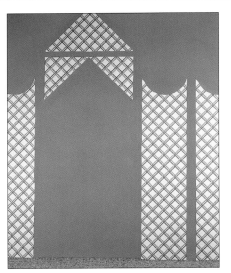

1 The trellis consists of a central pergola and a scalloped fence. A width of wallpaper is equal to a pergola or two fence sections. Determine the fence height and cut out enough sections to go around the walls. Leave 5cm/2in between each section. Cut a scallop at the top of each fence using a dinner plate as a template.

2 Cut two triangles from the paper to form the pergola. The base of the triangle is the width of the paper and the pergola has a central height of 25.5cm/10in. Paste one triangle above the height of the fence. Cut the other triangle in half and paste these pieces, at right-angles, under the first triangle.

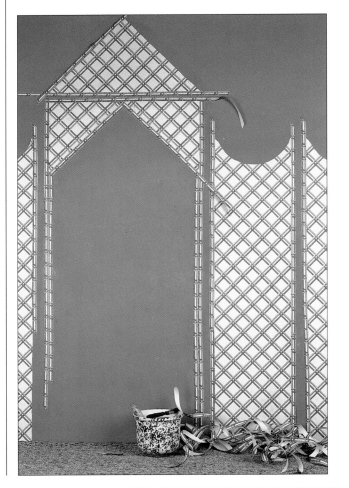

3 Cut narrow border strips from the remaining wallpaper and use to finish the edges all around the fences and the pergola. Extend the border strips from the two small triangles to form the support "legs". Clip the border strip every 12mm/1/2in across its width to ease around the curves.

Botanical Print Cupboard

I found these flower prints in a dusty secondhand store. Look out for old greetings cards or postcards which would be equally effective.

MATERIALS

flower prints

cupboard

scissors

wrapping paper

paper paste

household paint brush

varnish

Hints

Protect the final decoration with at least three or four layers of spray-on varnish for a quick result.

1 Cut out the flower prints to a size most suited to your cupboard door fronts. These doors are long and thin so I have trimmed my prints accordingly. Cut out flower and leaf patterns from the wrapping papers. Paste flower prints in position.

2 Paste a leafy edge around all the flower prints to create a border. Make sure you completely cover the cut edge of the flower prints so there is no white paper showing. Make sure that the paste is applied right up to the edge of the leaves.

3 Position and paste more leafy motifs together with small clusters of flowers on the remainder of the doors until you achieve a pleasing design. Experiment with unusual arrangements for an attractive look before pasting the motifs in their final positions. Varnish.

Display Shelves

Hung with little raffia tassels, these neat display shelves look attractive and provide useful storage for a kitchen or bathroom.

MATERIALS

stiff cardboard

craft knife

ruler

pencil

scissors

gummed paper strip

handmade paper

wallpaper paste

brush

corrugated paper

brown paper

bradawl

raffia

masking tape

Hints

Decorate the shelving with beads or feathers as an alternative to the raffia.

1 Decide on the length and width of the shelving. Cut a piece of cardboard to this size plus an extra 7.5cm/3in all round for the depth of the shelves. With a closed pair of scissors score the cardboard 7.5cm\3in in from each edge. Cut out squares at each corner. Fold up the sides and tape together with gummed paper strip.

2 Cut strips of cardboard 7.5cm/3in wide for the shelves. Use a ruler to mark their positions, keeping them an even distance apart and varying their lengths and arrangement for a more interesting look. Fix the shelves in place using the gummed strip along all edges for added support.

3 Measure the spaces between the shelves and cut strips of handmade paper to fit these areas. Use paste to stick in position. This distinctive paper with its fern leaf detail is perfect for the shelving.

4 Cover the outside of the unit with corrugated paper starting with the shortest sides. Cut the paper a little longer than these sides to wrap around the corners. Make 7.5cm/3in cuts in the paper at the points where the shelves meet the sides so you can tuck the paper inside easily.

5 Line the internal shelves with brown paper covering above and below each shelf. Cut the paper to the exact size as there should be no overlap along these edges. Where one shelf meets another, snip the paper and smooth neatly into the corners. Paste down.

6 Make two holes in the top of the unit using the bradawl. Thread a length of plaited raffia through the holes, wrapping the ends with tape to make threading easier. Knot and fray the ends.

Office Storage Boxes

Most office storage boxes are grey and boring, but attractively covered boxes could brighten your working day.

MATERIALS

files, boxes

wallpapers

pencil

ruler

scissors

paste

brush

craft knife

Hints

You will need a length of wallpaper approx. 1.5m/6ft long to cover a box and its lid. The steps show you how to cover a box base. Simply repeat the procedure, on a smaller scale, for the lid.

1 Place the box on the wrong side of the wallpaper and mark its position. The paper should be large enough to cover the box sides plus a narrow turning to the inside edge. Cut the paper to fit, allowing an extra 5cm/2in flap on the shorter side edges to wrap around the corners.

2 Remove the box and apply paste to the wallpaper. Place the box on the wallpaper using the pencil marks to register the position. Glue the shorter side pieces first including the flap. Follow with the longer sides, pasting over the flap to neaten.

3 If you cover an index opening, locate its centre with your fingers and pierce with a craft knife. Determine the position of the four corners. Use a sharp blade to make a cross in the middle, cutting the points outwards to touch the four corners. Fold the flaps back and cut off.

Picture Frame

If you want to surround simple photographs or pictures, this is an attractive idea for a unique and inexpensive frame.

MATERIALS

craft knife

cardboard

bradawl or skewer

scissors

paste

handmade paper

brush

paper fasteners

coiled paper ribbon

masking tape

Hints

To use as a picture frame for a wall, simply extend the paper ribbon between two top corners to form a hanging loop.

1 Cut four cardboard frame pieces each 5x30cm/2x12in. Place together in a square formation so that each corner overlaps the next creating a cross shape. Using the bradawl punch a hole through the centre of each of the four corner joins.

2 Again using the bradawl, punch a pattern of holes down each side of the frame keeping the holes at least 1cm/3/8in apart. Cut and paste handmade paper over the front of the frame pieces, making sure that the paper overlaps to the back.

3 Push the bradawl through the holes in the cardboard to pierce the handmade paper covering each piece. Insert a paper fastener into each hole (apart from those at the corners) for decoration. Flatten the fastener tabs at the back. Neaten the back of the frame with a strip of handmade paper.

4 Assemble the four sides together as shown, aligning the four holes at the corners. Re-emphasise these four holes with another twist of the bradawl. Thread with a piece of coiled ribbon, knotting at the front and back. Leave approx 5cm/2in at the front before cutting. Fan out the ribbon.

5 Cut a square of cardboard to cover the back of the frame and secure with masking tape. To make a stand for the frame, simply cut out a cardboard support for the back and attach it to the frame with tape. Cover with handmade paper if you wish.

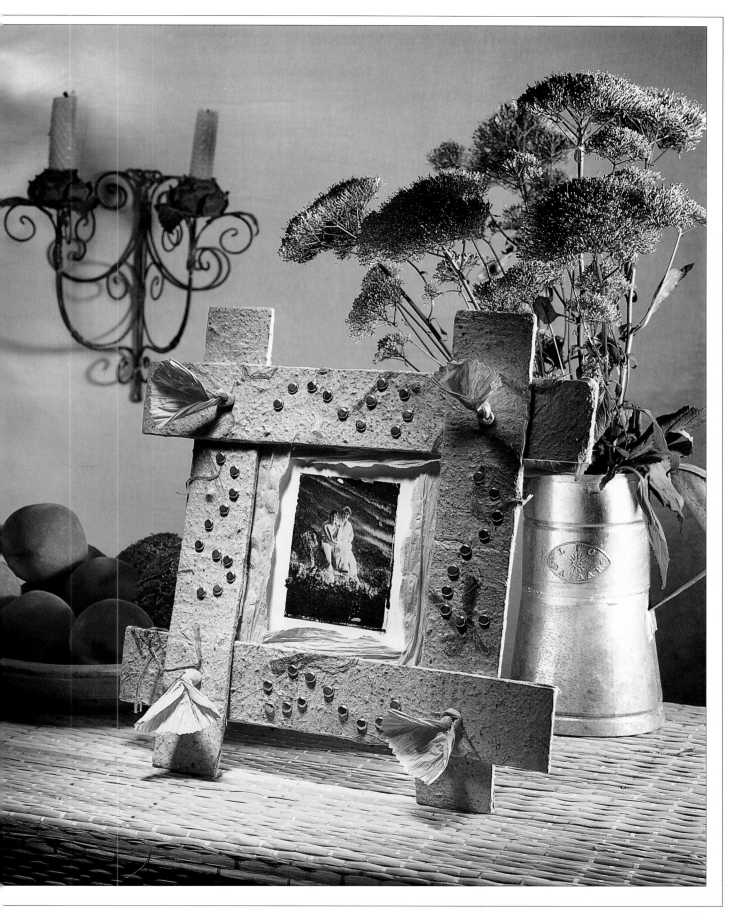

Paper Blind

This blind will fold upwards like a Roman Blind because of the way the string is knotted to the loops. Hang the blind with the rushes at the front.

MATERIALS

tape measure

pencil

soft handmade paper

scissors

beach mat

glue

needle

raffia

string

wooden batten

brass eyelets

Hints

Secure a wooden batten to the top of your window frame. Fix two brass eyelets to the bottom edge in corresponding positions to the loops on the blind.

1 Measure the window for which the blind is intended. Transfer the width and height measurements onto the paper and cut out to these dimensions. Sew sheets of paper together if one sheet is not large enough. Pull separate rush strands from the beach mat.

2 Glue the rush strands across the width of paper at regular intervals. The gaps should be a minimum of 10cm/4in apart. Thread the needle with raffia and stitch over the strands to secure them to the paper. Occasionally sew through a strand twice for extra security.

3 Make raffia tassels and sew to the ends of the rushes. Tie string loops around each rush strand, 7.5cm/3in from each side of the blind. Starting at the bottom of the blind, thread string through each loop, knotting at alternate loops, and finally through the eyelets on the wooden batten attached to the window frame.

Child's
Lampshade

This decoration uses the old-fashioned technique of folding and cutting paper, but I've replaced the traditional doll with this jaunty chicken.

MATERIALS

photocopied chicken

black cartridge paper

pencil

scissors

glue

paper lampshade

needle

thread

Hints

Cut a row of complete chickens - no halves - and position on the lampshade at the most convenient height.

1 Enlarge our chicken shape by 200% on a photocopier to quadruple its size. Cut a strip of black paper to the width of the chicken's height. Draw around the chicken, then concertina fold the paper ensuring that the chicken's leg and beak overlap the folds.

2 Cut around the chicken shape through two or three folds of paper at one time. Use the last cut-out chicken shape as the cutting line for the next three folds. Repeat the process until you have cut out enough chickens to go around the shade.

3 Join the last chicken to the first with a little glue and position this band onto the lampshade. Sew through the top of each chicken head and tail using a loose stitch to secure it in place. Fit the shade in place.

Picture Rosettes

These look particularly attractive
if two or more rosettes are used
to hang a group of pictures.

MATERIALS

coloured paper ribbons
scissors
sticky tape
coiled paper ribbon
glue
mounting pads
picture hooks

Hints

Use different types and weights of paper
to vary the look. Tissue paper would
look interesting used with a textured
handmade paper.

1 Cut two tails for the rosette from coloured paper ribbon. I cut a wide paper ribbon in half lengthways to give two narrower widths which were better suited to the size of my picture frame. Snip the ribbon tails into a V shape.

2 For the outer and inner rosettes concertina fold a 10cm/4in wide ribbon and a 7.5cm/3in wide ribbon respectively. Pleat the outer rosette at least eight times and the inner at least ten. Hold centrally with your thumb and forefinger and pull the outer edges together. Tape the edges closed.

3 Glue the inner rosette to the top of the outer rosette. Snip small pieces from the coiled paper ribbon to make a centre for the rosette. Glue in place. Use the mounting pads to secure the ribbon tails to the wall and then the rosette. Position the picture over the ribbon tails. Hang from small picture hooks.

Panelled Door

If you have a featureless door but like the look of a panelled one, you can create the effect with paper.

MATERIALS

tape measure

coloured sugar paper

pencil

ruler

scissors

paste

craft knife

speckled paper

varnish

household paint brush

Hints

If the door has been painted with an oil-based paint, you will need to attach the paper with PVA glue mixed with 50% water.

1 Measure the width of the door and divide into seven. One-seventh is the width of the borders, two-sevenths is the width of a panel. From the coloured paper cut three border strips the length of the door and three strips the width of the door.

2 Measure and mark the position of the four panels. Paste two long and two short strips to cover the outer edges of the door. The remaining long and short strips form a cross in the middle of the four panels. Trim away the excess paper where it overlaps at the corners.

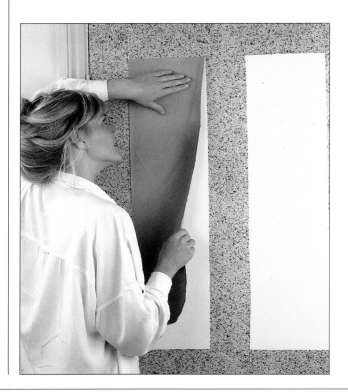

3 Draw the measurements of the panel on the speckled paper and use a ruler and sharp craft knife to cut out. Paste carefully onto the door, making sure they butt neatly against the vertical and horizontal borders. Coat with at least three layers of varnish to protect.

CHAPTER 4
DÉCOUPAGE

Today the designs in wrapping papers are almost as wonderful and varied as any fabric design - what's more they seem to change with each season as in the fashion industry. I have used lots of wonderful wrapping papers in this chapter. They are fantastic for all types of découpage, whether you cut a single print from one sheet or use lots of different sheets. Don't limit yourself to the familiarity of a jewellery box or firescreen for your projects, however pretty they are. I'll show you how to transform a boring, old chair into a talking point with a bundle of gift tags! And the humble kitchen table has been given a new lease of life with an attractive fruit border cut from nothing more exotic than two sheets of wrapping paper!

Shell Placemats

I used old wooden placemats for this project, but you could make them from cork or even thick cardboard.

MATERIALS

place mats

spray paint

shell patterned paper

scissors

plasticine

PVA glue

varnish

Hints

It is possible to use oil-based paint to cover the place mats but allow a longer drying time.

1 Cover the surface of the old placemats using the spray paint. You may find that you need several coats to obliterate all the design underneath. Spray the paint evenly, building up thin layers and allowing it to dry between coats.

2 Cut out the shells from the paper. If you cannot find a shell paper, fish or fruit prints cut from wrapping paper or magazines would look just as effective. Position the shells on the mat securing with plasticine until you are happy with the arrangement.

3 Remove the plasticine and glue the shells onto the place mat using PVA glue. Leave to dry then seal and protect with at least three layers of varnish. Repeat until you have completed all the placemats. Remember these are wipe-clean only.

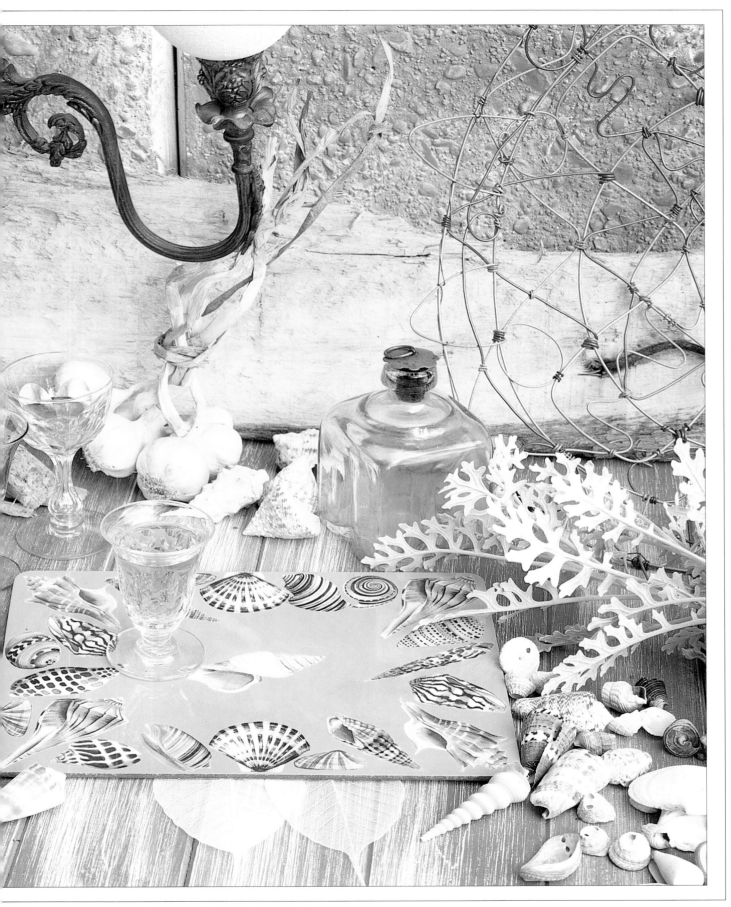

Music
Manuscript
Cabinet

Look for lots of different material related to music or pictures of musical instruments.

MATERIALS

painted cabinet

music manuscript (sheet music)

wallpaper paste

household paint brush

ruler

pencil

printed musical material

PVA glue

sepia watercolour

artist's brush

varnish

Hints

If you have just one sheet of music, use a photocopier to produce enough copies to cover the panels.

1 Cover the panels on the outside of the door with the sheet music using wallpaper paste. If there aren't any panels on your cabinet, draw a border at least 7.5cm/3in from the sides of the door to create a fake central panel.

2 Cut out all the material that you would like to use on the cabinet. It's a good idea to cut more than you need so you can move the prints around adding or eliminating pieces until you are happy with the design. Glue the pieces with PVA.

3 Tint the whole collage with sepia watercolour diluted with 50% water to give an appearance of age and antiquing to the cabinet and ensure that even designs printed on the whitest papers are more subtle. Varnish to protect.

Games Board

Stick this board permanently to the top of a small side table and use as a games board whenever you have the inclination.

MATERIALS

set square or ruler
pencil
square board cut from MDF
three colours of marbled paper
craft knife
PVA glue
brush
varnish

Hints

Use strong colour contrasts for the marbled paper squares so the checkerboard effect is more eye-catching.

1 Use a set square or ruler and pencil to divide the board. First draw a thin border all around the four sides. Then divide the internal space evenly into 64 squares, each side of the board having eight squares. Cut two colours of paper into 32 squares to these measurements. Glue in place, alternating the colours in each row.

2 Cut thin border strips from the third paper and glue in position around the sides of the board, taking care not to overlap the paper squares. Finish with a coloured square stuck over the border in each corner. Put the same colour in opposite corners. Varnish to protect.

Gift Tag Chair

This is a delightful way to pattern a chair and as there are so many pretty gift tags available you could have a different design on each chair.

MATERIALS

craft knife

10 gift tags

masking tape

chair

PVA glue

white emulsion paint

household paint brush

cotton cloth

varnish

Hints

I find it easier to varnish the chair upside down, starting with the legs. Leave to dry before turning over to finish.

1 Using a craft knife, cut the excess white card from around the design on the gift tag. Cut around the hole for the cotton tie, if the design allows. If you are sticking the tags on a coloured chair, it is important to cut away most of the white card.

2 Form a circle with the tag cut-outs to fit the seat of your chair. Carefully tuck each cut-out end under the next so the circle is complete. Hold secure with masking tape, then transfer to the chair. Glue in place. Remove the tape. Glue one tag to the chair back.

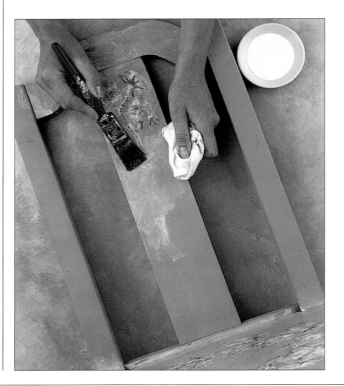

3 Colour-wash the chair with a coat of emulsion paint thinned with 50% water. Apply with the household paint brush. Use the soft cloth to wipe away a little of the paint while it is still wet to give a slightly faded look to the chair. Allow to dry, then protect with two layers of varnish.

Patchwork Border

This is simple idea, but as with fabric patchwork the key to success lies in the preparation. So take time when cutting out the diamond shapes before you start to paste.

MATERIALS

cartridge paper

dinner plate

pencil

ruler

protractor

scissors

four co-ordinating wallpapers

masking tape

craft knife

wallpaper paste

paste brush

cotton cloth

Hints

Make a simple cartridge paper template by drawing around a dinner plate. Divide the template in half with a pencil and ruler. Set a protractor along one straight edge and mark off three 60 degree angles on each half. Join the points that touch the curved edge of the circle with a ruler. Cut out the three basic diamond shapes as shown.

1 Place four pieces of wallpaper on top of each other, keeping the edges even, and hold together with masking tape. Position the three diamond-shaped templates across the width of paper, side by side. Draw parallel lines across the top and bottom. Once a pattern is established for drawing the diamonds, repeat the formation of rows across the paper and cut out the diamond shapes.

2 Use the diamond shapes in various wallpaper patterns to plot the shape of the stars. Work on a flat surface to familiarise yourself with the construction of the pattern before you start pasting to the wall. You will see that as the star touches the dado rail some diamonds need to be halved to fit.

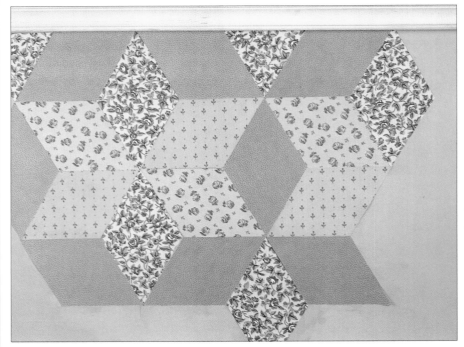

3 Paste the diamonds and stick these to the wall butting the edges up to each other and smoothing them out with a cotton cloth. You will find the patchwork effect takes shape quickly as you start to paste the stars and a regular pattern builds up.

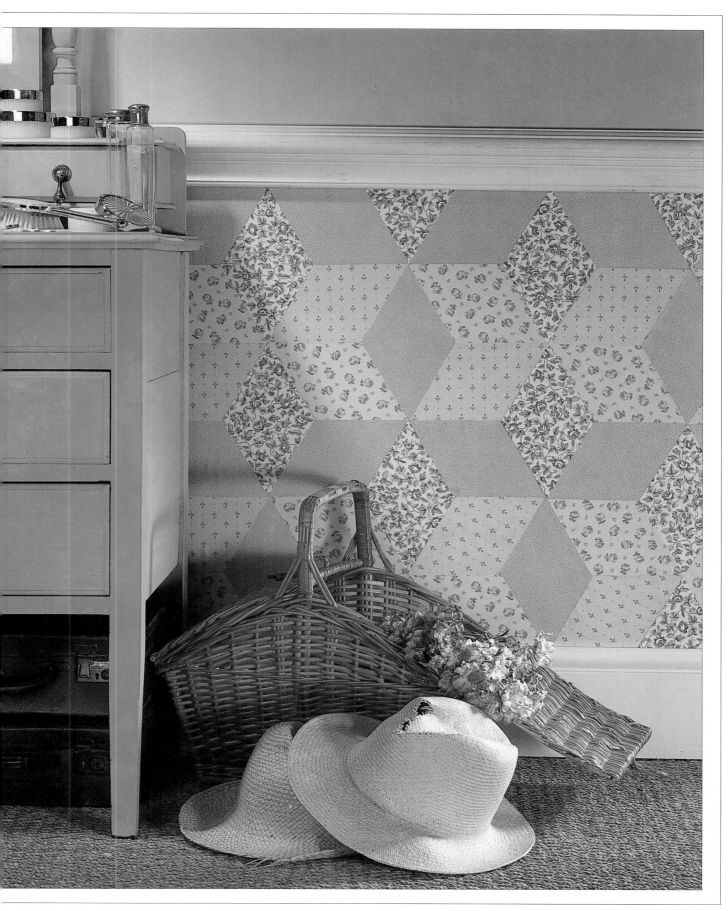

Kitchen Table

This decoration is a delightful way to pattern an old or scratched table.

MATERIALS

fruit wrapping paper

scissors

PVA glue

chalk string

household brush

emulsion paint

varnish

Hints

If you are decorating an unpainted table prepare the area to take the découpage by rubbing the surface with a fine-grade sandpaper to roughen the surface.

1 Cut out the fruit images from the wrapping papers. You may have to cut images from a few papers to give you enough fruits to go all the way around the edge of the table. Remember to include any leaves that may be a part of the design.

2 Use the PVA to stick the fruits around the edge of the table to form a deep border. Ensure that you paste right up to the edges of each fruit and leaves. For a smooth finish press the fruits onto the table being careful not to overlap the paper.

3 To accentuate the découpage edge I have painted a dilute layer of emulsion over the border. If you don't have a steady hand mark out the border with white chalk. To do this tie chalk to a length of string measuring the diameter of the table, less the width of the border. Hold the free end under the thumb in the table centre and pulling the string taut mark out the circle in chalk. Dilute the paint 50/50 with water and use a wide brush to quickly cover the area. While the paint is still wet remove the paint from the surface of the découpage and some from between the fruits for an attractive edge. Varnish to seal surface.

Firescreen

If you don't have a fireplace you could make a feature of this screen simply by placing it in a corner of the room.

MATERIALS

hardboard base

fretsaw

scissors

floral wrapping paper

pencil

household paint brush

emulsion paint

PVA glue

strong adhesive

varnish

Hints

Place a sheet of wrapping paper on the hardboard. Use its height and width as a guide around which to draw an elongated circle. This may be wider than the paper at some points. Draw a wavy line through this and cut out with a fretsaw.

1 Cut out lots of individual flower and fruit motifs from the wrapping paper. If the flowers are printed against a dark background, don't worry too much about trimming right up to the edges. Keep one sheet whole for the background.

2 Paint the back of the screen and a narrow border around the front with emulsion paint. Glue the whole sheet of paper to the front of the screen, trimming around the fruit and flowers motifs at the top edge so they fit into the curves. Stick on individually cut flowers to fill the gaps.

3 Use tiny flowers and butterflies cut from the rest of the wrapping paper to add interest. Make a stand for the screen by cutting two 90 degree triangles from the excess hardboard. Coat with emulsion paint. Glue to the back of the screen with strong adhesive. Protect the front of the screen with three coats of varnish.

Marbled
Table Top

Cover an old round table top with
these marbled papers for an
effective marquetry look.

MATERIALS

table

thin paper for template

pencil

craft knife

scissors

four colours of marbled paper

tape measure

PVA glue

varnish

Hints

It's a good idea to cut the paper on layers
of newspaper to protect the surface of
the table.

1   Tape the thin paper template to the table. Draw, then cut around the circumference using a sharp craft knife. Fold the circle in half, then in half again. Repeat until there are sixteen segments. Cut out one segment and remove it to use as a template.

2   Cut out segments from each of the coloured marbled papers. Use a pencil to mark off two sections at the top of the template segment, approx 5cm/2in apart. Cut out. Use these three new templates to cut out all the coloured marbled paper segments in the same way.

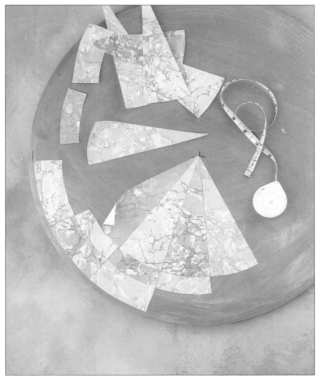

3   Using a tape measure, draw two lines across the diameter of the table, then divide into 16 segments. Use the PVA to glue down the marbled paper segments, alternating the colours to make a pattern like the one we have created. Seal and protect with four layers of varnish.

Decorated Headboard

I have used offcuts from rolls of wallpaper to make this découpage headboard. Look for faded ochre and sepia colours for a more romantic feel.

MATERIALS

headboard

wallpaper offcuts

scissors

wallpaper paste

household paint brush

PVA glue

varnish

Hints

Strip any fabric from your old headboard and decorate with emulsion paint. Or cut a new headboard from MDF, paint, then transfer the fittings from the old headboard.

1 Cut out all the large groups of flowers and the largest individual flowers from the wallpaper. Position on the headboard, moving them around until you have a pleasing arrangement. Don't worry about gaps, these can be filled in later. Paste the shapes down.

2 Cut out the smaller individual flowers and leaves and paste these into the gaps. Use PVA glue on those flowers that need to overlap the already pasted flowers, for a more permanent bonding. You may find you need lots of these smaller pieces.

3 Cut out all the finer detailed pieces of the wallpaper like buds and leaf stems. This may seem quite tedious and time consuming, but the end result is worth it. Stick these all around the headboard filling in the gaps. Protect with two or three layers of varnish.

Cherub Clock

This clock has such a stunning shape, like a grand carriage clock, that it can take pride of place on your mantelpiece.

MATERIALS

dinner plate	PVA glue diluted 50/50 with water
polyboard	craft knife
pencil/pen	wrapping paper
ruler	tea bag
wallpaper paste	skewer
music manuscript	clock mechanism
cherub patterned paper	masking tape

Hints

Polyboard is much easier to use than any of the alternatives. If it is not available, use hardboard instead.

1 Position a large dinner plate centrally on the polyboard. Mark out a border measuring 72x20.5cm/28x8in at the base of the plate. Draw around the plate and gently curve the two sides outwards to meet the edge of the border, creating a classic carriage clock shape.

2 Cut around your outline. Paste the music manuscript to the centre of the clock. Don't worry about covering the whole clock face as the cherubs will overlap and form a border. Cut the cherubs from the paper and position them around the clock. Stick down with PVA glue.

3 When the glue is dry, use a sharp craft knife to cut around the cherub details at the outer edge of the clock, keeping as much detail as you can. Cut two polyboard triangles and cover with wrapping paper for the back support.

4 Wash the surface of the clock with a cooled, wet teabag to age the appearance. Punch a hole through the centre of the clock with a skewer. Push the clock mechanism through the hole and secure at the back with a little tape. Secure the back supports in the same way.

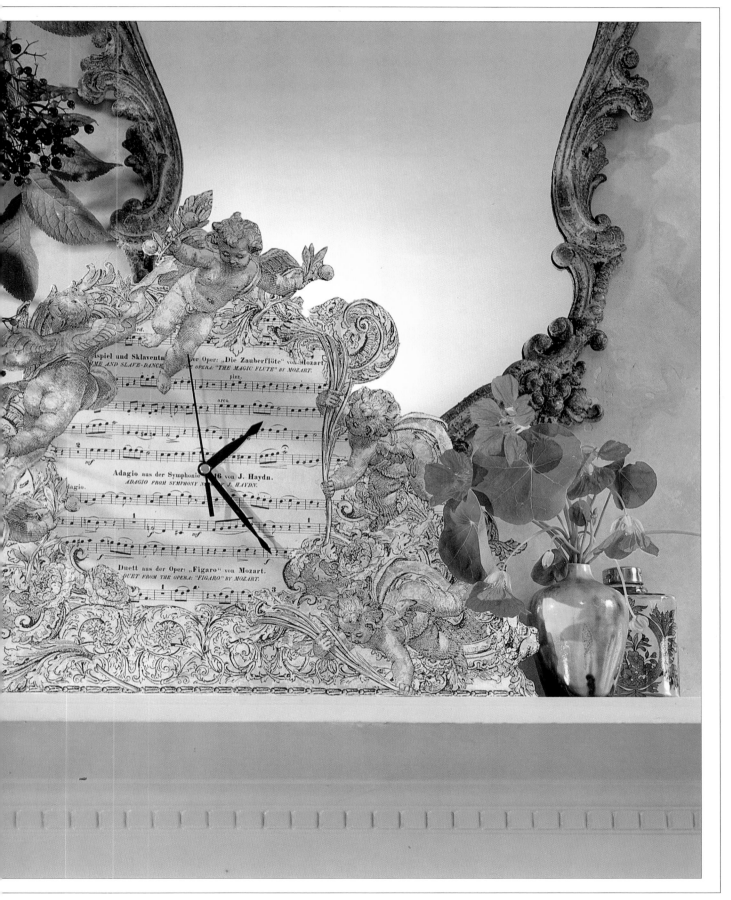

Rose-covered Box

I love the simplicity of this patterned jewellery box. The whole design is cut from one sheet of wrapping paper with all its elements rearranged.

MATERIALS

wrapping paper

scissors

wooden box

emulsion paint

household paint brush

PVA glue

craft knife

varnish

Hints

Look through seed catalogues or gardening magazines for other designs to pattern your box.

1 Select the paper or prints you would like for your box. I have chosen an old-fashioned rose design that reminds me of a cottage garden, which is ideal for my traditional bedroom scheme. Cut out all the elements you need from the paper.

2 If the box isn't painted, then colour it with at least two coats of emulsion, allowing the coats to dry between each application. Position the cut roses around the lid of the box until you form a design that you are happy with. Stick down with a little PVA glue.

3 Choose a smaller, more detailed print and use as a narrow border around the outside of the box, taking care to glue right up to the edges. Score across the opening of the box with a sharp knife if the flowers overlap this edge. Varnish to protect.

ACKNOWLEDGEMENTS

The publishers would like to thank the following companies for
providing accessories for use in our photographs.
After Noaha, 121 Upper Street, Islington, London N.1
Laura Ashley, PO Box 19,Newton, Powys SY16 1DZ
and 6 St James Avenue, 10th Floor, Boston MA02116
Crucial Trading Co., 4 St Barnabas Street, London SW1
Graham & Green, 4 & 7 Elgin Crescent, London W11
Global Village, 247/249 Fulham Road, London SW3 6HY
Hallmark Cards, Station Road, Henley-on-Thames, Oxon RJ9 JLQ
Paperchase, 213 Tottenham Court Road, London W1P 9AF
Sanderson, 6 Cavendish Square, London W1
The National Trust, 36 Queen Anne's Gate, London SW1H 9AS
Tintawn Carpets Ltd, Claire House, Bridge Street, Leatherhead,
Surrey KT22 8BZ

GLOSSARY

Some of the terms used in this book may not be familiar to
American readers.
Here is a list of their US equivalents.

UK	US
A4 bond paper	8 x 10 typing paper
biscuit	cookie
blind	window shade
bradawl	awl
cling film	plastic wrap
concertina fold	accordion pleat
craft knife	mat knife
dustbin	trash can
dust sheet	drop cloth
emulsion paint	latex
fretsaw	scroll saw
hardboard	masonite
MDF	particle board
matt finish	flat finish
muslin	cheesecloth
music manuscript	sheet music
plasticine	modeling clay
polyboard	sheet styrofoam
PVA glue	craft glue
set square	carpenter's square
sieve	strainer
sticky tape	cellophane tape
sugar paper	construction paper
sweets	candy
tea plate	luncheon plate
whisk	eggbeater
wirewool	steel wool

GIFT WRAPPING & GREETINGS CARDS

GIFT WRAPPING

& GREETINGS CARDS

*Creative ideas for personalizing
gifts and cards*

Edited by Lydia Darbyshire

APPLE

A QUINTET BOOK

Published by The Apple Press
6 Blundell Street
London N7 9BH

ISBN 1-85076-734-3

Reprinted in 1998

This book was designed and produced by
Quintet Publishing Limited
6 Blundell Street
London N7 9BH

Creative Director: Richard Dewing
Designer: Michael Head
Project Editor: Clare Hubbard
Editor: Lydia Darbyshire

Typeset in Great Britain by
Central Southern Typesetters, Eastbourne
Manufactured in China by
Regent Publishing Services Ltd
Printed in China by Leefung-Asco Printers Ltd

Material in this book previously appeared in
Creative Christmas Crafts, editor Alison Wormleighton,
Creative Nature Crafts, Alison Jenkins with text by Tessa Eveleigh,
Discover Rubber Stamping by Terry McEwan and Jenny Hume,
Giftwrappings for Every Occasion by Gill Dickinson,
Make it with Paper by Paul Jackson and Vivien Frank,
Pop-up Greetings Cards by Mike Palmer,
The Silk Flower Arranger's Companion by Pat Reeves,
Start a Craft Christmas Crafts by Alison Jenkins,
Start a Craft Greetings Cards by Sharon McSwiney,
Start a Craft Stencilling by Jamie Sapsford and Betsy Skinner

CONTENTS

Introduction

The cost of shop-bought cards and gift-wrapping paper
seems to increase almost daily, and how
frustrating it is to spend almost as
much on paper and ribbon as on
the gift itself, only to be
disappointed with the end
result. This book
contains everything you
need to know to create the
perfect wrapping every time.
Not only does it show how to wrap
parcels of every imaginable size and
shape, but it also explains how to make and
decorate paper. There are instructions for making gift
tags and dozens of unusual cards, including cut-outs and
pop-ups for every occasion.

8

There seem to be more and more occasions for exchanging gifts and cards – Christmas, birthdays, Easter, Halloween, weddings, Valentine's Day, Mother's Day . . . the list goes on and on. In the pages that follow you will find a wealth of inspirational ideas and techniques for creating dozens of different looks for presents and greeting cards. Whether you need to wrap a gift for a dedicated gardener (cover the wrapping paper with dried leaves and berries) create a fun gift for a child (make a giant pencil and fill it with novelty pens and pencils) or whether you want to make a card to celebrate a wedding, there is an original idea to delight everyone.

Handmade cards are often kept for far longer than commercially made ones, not simply because they are so much more personal than shop-bought ones and show that you have spent time and trouble thinking about the occasion and the recipient. Handmade cards are often little works of art in their own right, and they may even be kept and framed as an original picture. Many contemporary craft workers and artists produce their own greetings cards, to sell and to give to their own relatives and friends, because they can be a unique form of expression.

Making greetings cards enables you to achieve excellent results in a short space of time and with very few materials. Because the scale is small and the techniques are, usually, simple to master, it is possible to produce something that looks professional without any specific art training. Many of the projects described in this book require nothing more than a few paints, some colored card, a crayon or pen, and your imagination. You can use sponges or your fingers instead of paintbrushes and allow your designs to evolve as you explore the different techniques. Some of the techniques described can be adapted for multiple use, so you can, if you wish, produce many cards at a time. Others are more involved and require the use of several techniques, but the instructions given will enable you to create individual, very special cards.

The emphasis throughout is on using natural and recycled materials whenever possible to create beautiful gift wrappings. Often there is no need to buy expensive ribbons, paper, and gift tags when you can find an amazing range of materials and inspiration all around you – in the garden, on the beach, or among the things you might otherwise throw away.

Keep a box for your collection of gift-wrapping accessories, from old buttons to odds and ends of ribbon and string. Whenever you take a walk along a beach or in a forest, keep an eye out for interesting natural objects, such as shells, driftwood, seaweed, leaves, pine cones, berries, and flowers. Keep old cards and pretty wrapping papers – you can cut out motifs from them for your new designs.

Most of the projects and techniques can be enjoyed by the whole family. Children will love making their own wrapping paper and tags with potato printing, paint spattering, and simple stencils. If you use recycled materials – decorating plain brown paper, for example – these techniques are also inexpensive. If you run out of ideas, simply look through the pages that follow and you are sure to come up with something original.

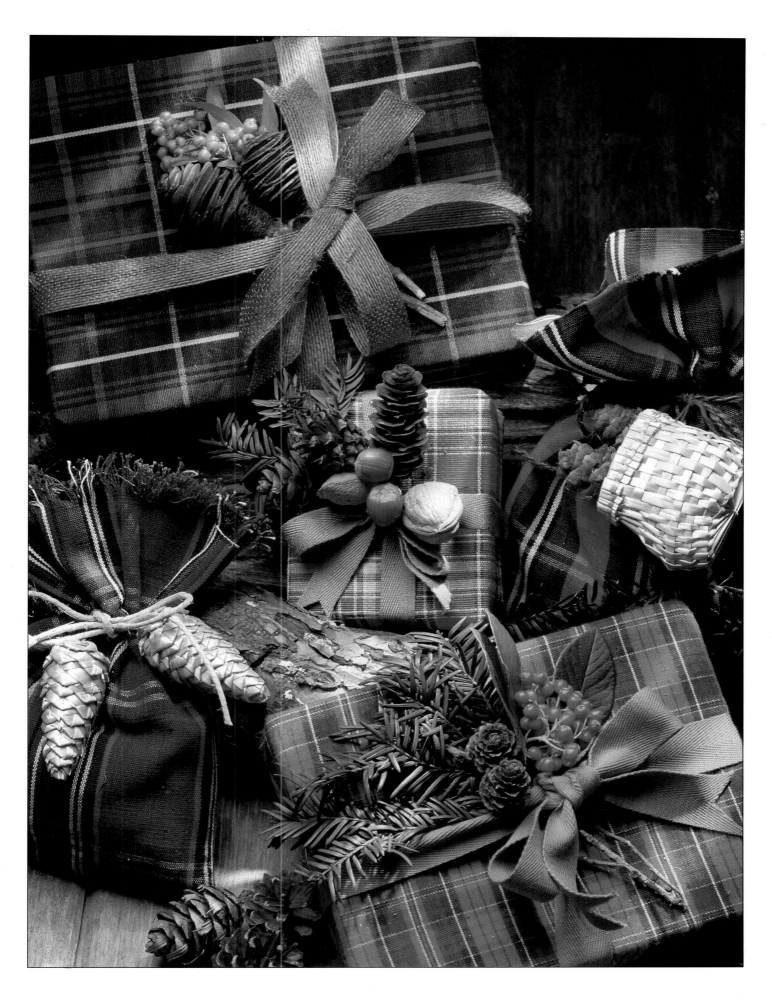

Materials and Equipment

PAINTS AND INKS

Designer gouache, which is available in tubes or small pots, is water-soluble. It gives an even, matt finish, is fast drying, and is easily mixed to create new shades, although a huge range is offered by the manufacturers. It is readily available from art shops and good stationery suppliers.

Ornamental sprays, which include gold and silver metallic spray paints and automobile spray paints, can be bought in hardware stores, art shops, and automobile repair stores. The paint is available in cans. When you use a spray paint, it is a good idea to make a "spray booth" from a large cardboard box. Always use sprays in a well-ventilated room, or, even better, work outside. You may have to practice to avoid applying too much paint at a time.

Block printing ink is water-soluble and is sold in tubes. It is used straight from the tube – there is no need to dilute it with water. It is also possible to obtain oil-based block printing inks, but these take much longer to dry. The inks are available in a range of colors, but black tends to give the best and most consistent results. The ink is available in art shops.

Drawing ink is available in small bottles or jars. It is water-soluble and can be applied with brushes, although you should wash them thoroughly immediately after use, or with steel-nib dipping pens. Various colors are available, including metallic gold and silver. It can be bought from art or craft shops.

Wax crayons and candles are useful resist materials. The crayons intended for children, which are available from art shops and stationery stores, are ideal, because they are inexpensive, non-toxic, and available in a wide range of colors and sizes. White household candles are available from hardware stores.

Glitter can be used to add sparkle to almost any design. Glitter glue (which has glitter in the adhesive solution) or loose glitter can be used. Glitter glue is applied directly to the design. Practice first on a scrap piece of card. It should be the kind of card that you are going to use for your finished item, and also test your paints or crayons as some of the glues will blot and smudge. Loose glitter is applied by putting small amounts of glue on the appropriate parts of the design and shaking the glitter over the image. Work over a large sheet of paper so that surplus glitter can be poured back into the container. Whichever method you use, allow the glue to dry before moving the card or trying to insert it in an envelope.

PENS AND PENCILS

You will find a selection of different pens, pencils, and crayons useful. A fine, permanent black drawing pen, a black, water-soluble marker pen, a selection of ordinary felt- or fiber-tipped pens, and some gold and silver markers are all valuable additions to your equipment. You will also need some pencils, including a general-purpose HB pencil, a softer 4B, for transferring designs, and some inexpensive colored pencils, which are always useful for adding small decorative details.

ADHESIVES

One of the most convenient and tidiest of adhesives is a glue stick, of which there are several proprietary brands. They are all solid blocks of adhesive in a plastic tube, and they are particularly useful for bonding pieces of paper when only a small amount of adhesive is required or when you need to apply adhesive in a small, difficult-to-get-at area. They make it easy to control the amount of glue you apply and are especially suitable for children to use.

Many adhesives are sold in tubes, and they tend to be stronger than the adhesive in glue sticks. They are, therefore, necessary for sticking thicker papers and cards and for attaching non-paper items. Make sure you use them in a well-ventilated room.

A useful all-purpose glue is PVA adhesive, which is a non-toxic, water-based glue. Although it is a milky white, it dries clear, and it is available in plastic bottles and tins from craft shops and hardware stores. Excess glue can be removed by gently rubbing it off the paper with your finger. It can be applied with a brush, but you must wash the brush thoroughly in warm water immediately after use. For large pieces of paper a plastic spatula is useful for giving even coverage. PVA adhesive is also suitable for bonding fabrics, and if you are using fine or delicate fabrics, dilute the adhesive before use.

Double-sided adhesive tape is a useful alternative to glue and is essential for precisely folded parcels. It gives a strong, neat bond, and you can cut off small pieces and place them exactly where they are required. The tape is strong enough to hold card, and will also hold many non-paper items. Also useful are double-sided adhesive pads, which are small foam pads with a strong adhesive on both sides. They can be used for joining most materials, and are useful when you want to create a slightly three-dimensional effect.

A roll of masking tape is always useful to have. It can be easily removed from most surfaces without damaging them, and it is, therefore, invaluable for temporarily securing items, such as stencils, while you work. You can obtain special low-tack tape, which is especially easy to remove. Masking tape is available not only in stationery stores and art shops, but also many hardware shops, where it is often cheaper.

11

EQUIPMENT

If you are going to use a scalpel or craft knife for cutting out shapes you must protect your working surface. Although a piece of thick cardboard will do, you will find that the surface quickly becomes scored and makes it impossible to cut absolutely neat lines every time. A synthetic cutting mat, made from dense plastic, allows you to cut into it many times without damage. These mats are fairly expensive, but if you are going to use one regularly it will be more than worth the initial outlay. Most of the mats have grids superimposed on the surface, making it easy to position your ruler or set square to get perfect angles and straight lines.

There will be times when scissors are just not maneuverable enough, and you will need to cut out shapes with a craft knife or scalpel. Craft knives, which can also be used for general cutting of card, have snap-off, retractable blades, which are especially useful because you can be sure that you always have a sharp cutting tool. Craft knives in a range of styles are widely available. For safety, always store your craft knife with the blade retracted into the handle. Scalpels are sometimes needed for intricate cutting, and these are available from art shops. Protect the pointed blade with a cork. When you dispose of a scalpel blade or a section of blade from a craft knife, wrap it in a piece of masking tape and then in another piece of paper. Remember that all blades can be dangerous, but scalpel blades are especially sharp.

12

It is worth investing in at least two pairs of good, general-purpose scissors, which should, if you use them only for cutting paper, last for years. A pair of large scissors will be needed for cutting pieces of card, while smaller, pointed scissors are useful for cutting around curves and for snipping out smaller shapes. It is also possible to buy deckle-edged scissors, which will cut a random pattern and which are an easy, quick way of adding a feathered edge to paper and card. Pinking shears can be used to give a zigzag edge to paper and material. If you use fabric for any of the projects, make sure that you keep a special pair of scissors for all your needlework. Nothing blunts sewing scissors more quickly than using them to cut paper.

An ordinary paper punch will come in useful in all kinds of projects, but perhaps even more useful is a leather punch, which can be used to make single holes in card and fabric as well as paper. It has a revolving, star-shaped section that enables you to cut holes in up to six different sizes.

You will find that as well as an ordinary ruler, a metal rule is useful for cutting accurate edges with a craft knife. Always cut away from your body, and make sure that the card or paper to cut is resting on a cutting mat or thick piece of cardboard. A steel ruler will last longer than a wooden or plastic ruler. Some metal rulers have a rubber backing to stop them slipping when you press against them.

If you are going to use metal – perhaps as a stencil or as a decorative element in a card – you will need a pair of metal-ortin-snips. These are available from specialist jewelry tool suppliers, usually by mail order, or from good hardware stores. If you are not planning to cut metal regularly, you will find that a sharp pair of strong household scissors will do. A metal scriber, used to make designs in metal, will give a good, sharp line, but an old ball-point pen will often do just as well. It is a good idea to wear gloves when you are working with metal – the sharp edges can cause nasty cuts.

You will need several paintbrushes, which come in a bewildering range of qualities and sizes. Sable brushes can be very expensive, although if they are looked after and used only for paints, they will last for years. Synthetic brushes or ones with a mixture of real hair and synthetic materials are suitable for most work. You should aim to have at least one very fine brush, one medium sized one, and one broad, flat brush.

with ink pads, similar to those used in the office, although in a wide range of colors. Pigment inks, which are thick and rather creamy, are slow drying, but they are ideal for good, deep colors. Embossing inks are lightly tinted or colorless. They are slow-drying and are excellent for good embossed results. Embossing powders are available in metallic, transparent, and colored finishes. The powder is a heat-sensitive compound that solidifies when it is exposed to extreme temperatures. The easiest way of applying heat is by means of a hand-held paint stripper, but you can use an iron, an oven plate, or even a hot light bulb. Do not let the heat source come into contact with the embossing powder and do not over-heat the powder or it will look rather dull and unexciting.

Ordinary synthetic household sponges, torn or cut into pieces, can be used to apply paints. Use a separate piece of sponge for each color, and discard them after use.

Stencil brushes are available in a range of sizes and types. They have short, thick handles, and the brushes are cut off flat. You will find them in all good art shops.

Sometimes you will want to use a roller to spread ink evenly over a printing surface. Rollers are available from art shops and some hardware stores. After use, wash immediately in warm water. If you have used an oil-based ink, clean the roller with mineral (white) spirit.

Some of the projects use rubber stamps. When you are choosing your first stamp, look for a pattern or motif that can be used in several ways: craft and art shops stock an increasing range of designs, and some toy stores sell stamps representing characters from children's books, tv programs, and movies. You will find designs ranging from simple, individual letters to intricate patterns. The stamps are used

PAPER AND CARD

14

If you go into any art or craft shop you will find an enormous variety of papers and cards. Collect a range of colors, weights, and textures. Sugar paper, Ingres paper, and cartridge paper are all useful and come in a spectrum of colors. An inexpensive watercolor paper, which is suggested for use in some of the card projects, is useful because it will not break down when it is damp. This kind of paper also often has a slight texture, which can be exploited in your designs. Other useful papers and cards to keep are ordinary brown wrapping paper, tissue paper, foils, thin detail paper, gold and silver card, mounting board, inexpensive cardboard, and any unusually textured or handmade papers that you come across.

When you are preparing to make your own gift wraps and

cards, try to reuse paper whenever you can – tissue paper, brown paper, and even old gift-wrapping paper will all come in useful. Spattering paint onto crumpled tissue paper, for example, is a quick and easy way to create some original wrapping paper.

It is possible to obtain pre-cut card blanks. These are supplied and scored in a variety of sizes, colors, and types of card, and they can be used for many of the cards described. Many of them have pre-cut windows in ovals, hearts, squares, and rectangles, which are very useful. The cards are available in art and craft shops, and an even greater range is available by mail order. Look in the back of almost any craft magazine. However, you can easily cut out your own cards from a medium weight card, which gives you flexibility with both size and color. Choose a card that is heavy enough to stand upright but is not so thick that it will not fold neatly.

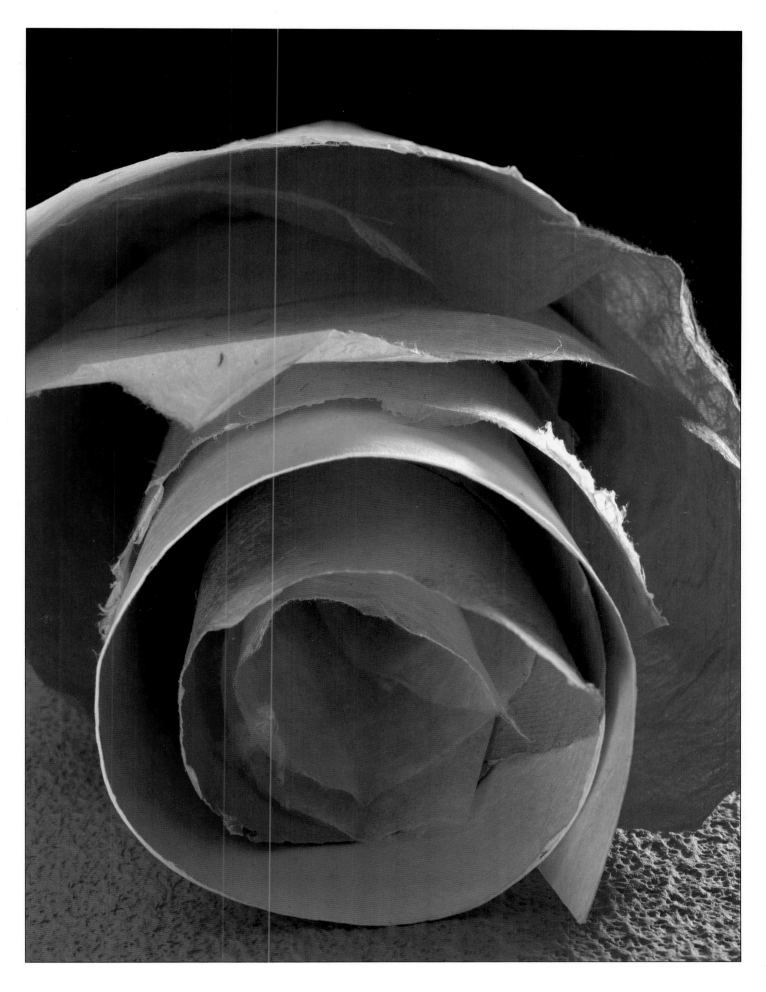

BIRTHDAYS

In this section are all kinds of ideas for decorating gifts of all shapes and sizes in unusual and attractive ways. There are also dozens of ideas for cards and gift tags. Many of these ideas can be used – with different materials, colors, and finishes – for other occasions than birthdays, and you will find suggestions in other sections of this book that can easily be translated into pretty, unusual, and original ideas for birthdays. There are several pop-up cards in this section. Few of them require any great degree of artistic skill, but they do require a little care and precision.

In addition to guidelines for creating the perfectly wrapped square or rectangular parcel every time, there are also some ingenious ideas for those gifts that sometimes refuse to be wrapped up neatly – bottles are always difficult, and many cosmetics come in odd shapes. Bags are easy to make and can look extremely decorative, and they have the advantage that you can make them fit any size or shape. Decorate them with handmade tags or add an unusual handle.

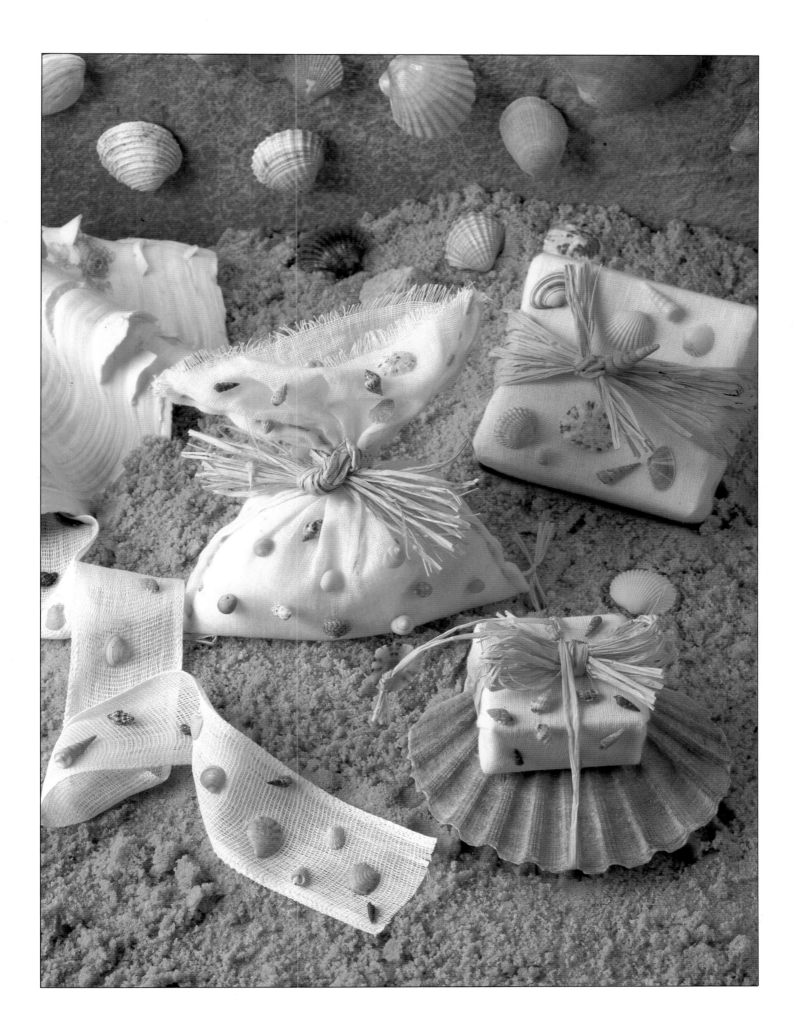

WRAPPING A BOX

Although a box is an easy shape to wrap, it's still important that the gift looks good.

  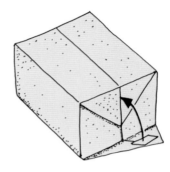

18

1. Cut the paper to fit the box. You will need an overlap at the top of about 10cm and two-thirds the box height at the sides. Fold down the top by 2cm from the edge. Center fold on the box and hold down with double-sided adhesive tape.

2. Center the box in the paper and press the folded edge against the box. Crease the side folds before pushing them in.

3. Fold up the triangular fold and fix with double-sided tape. Repeat at the other end of the box.

The delicate tissue papers have been decorated with relief fabric paints, which are easy to draw with and can be used straight from the tube. These papers have a seashore theme – shells and fish – but the technique can be used for abstract designs as well as pictorial ones.

TURN TURTLE

The technique used to make this appealing card requires very little equipment, but once you have made the "master" design you can make as many versions of it as you wish, using different colored wax crayons and different mounting card to create cards suitable for dozens of occasions. This motif was inspired by Australian Aboriginal designs, but the same method could be used for all kinds of patterns.

YOU WILL NEED

Tracing paper
Pencils (medium hard
  and very soft)
2 pieces white cartridge
  or sugar paper, 29 ×
  21cm
Scissors or craft knife
Clear, all-purpose
  adhesive or glue stick
Detail paper
Wax crayons: purple,
  blue
Maroon card, about
  23½ × 16cm

1. Place some tracing paper over the design and draw it with a medium hard pencil. Turn over the design and rub over the whole area with a soft (4B) pencil. Place the tracing paper, right side up, over the cartridge paper and go over the lines with a medium hard pencil so that the lines of the design are transferred to the paper.

Enlarge by 30% on a photocopier to trace at full size

2. Use sharp, pointed scissors or a craft knife to cut out the sections of the motifs.

3. Paste the cut-out shapes of the design onto a clean sheet of paper, including all the additional decorative features such as borders, stars, and swirls. Leave until the glue is dry.

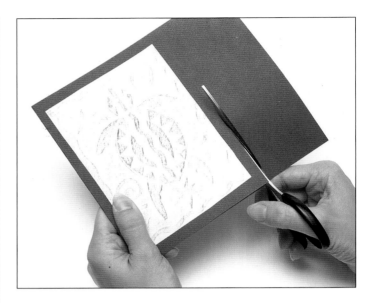

5. Trim the detail paper to size if necessary, and glue it to a larger piece of card of a contrasting color. Fold this to form a greeting card and trim to size.

4. Place some thin detail paper over the design and use a wax crayon to rub over the surface. Make sure that the detail paper is perfectly smooth and clean, and rub carefully over the surface in all directions to get an even cover. Use different colors for the different parts of the design.

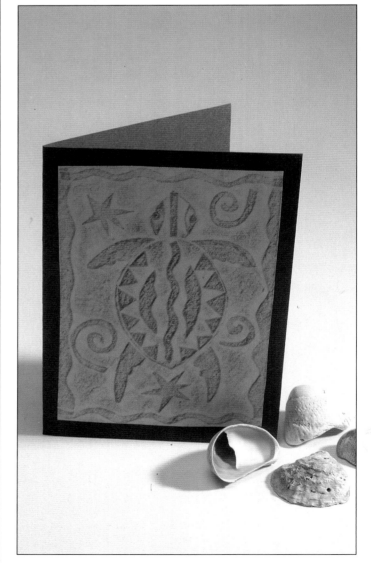

SUN AND MOON PRINTED CARD

Mono-printing is an easy-to-master technique, and you can use it to create one-off prints. A sun and moon motif was used for this card, which would be suitable for a birthday card, but this is one of the techniques that can be used for all kinds of patterns and designs. Linear designs are usually most successful, but you can add tone by applying pressure with your fingers to specific areas. The exciting thing about it is that, until you peel back the paper, you cannot tell exactly how the print is going to turn out.

YOU WILL NEED

Black block printing ink
Sheet of glass, about
  29 × 21cm
6cm ink roller
White sugar paper, about
  16 × 11cm

Pencil
Clear, all-purpose adhesive
Silver card
Maroon card, 20 × 15cm
Fine silver marker pen

Enlarge by 30% on a photocopier to trace at full size

2. Carefully place a piece of paper on the inked glass and use a sharp pencil to draw the design. The print will be the reverse of what you draw, and you can experiment with the pressure you apply to the pencil to give lighter and darker lines.

3. When the design is complete, carefully peel back the paper to reveal the print. Leave to dry. If you have used a water-soluble ink, this will take 20–30 minutes; if you have used an oil-based ink, leave for at least 2 hours.

1. Place a small amount of ink on the glass and use the roller to spread it evenly over the surface. Begin with a little ink, then gradually add more.

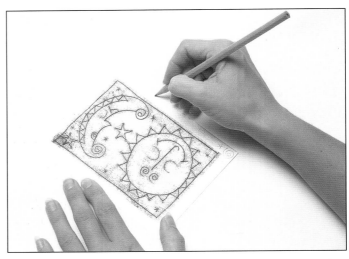

4. When the print is dry, glue it to a background of silver card, and trim to size, leaving a border of about 1.5cm all round.

22

5. If you wish, add further decoration by "scoring" patterns in the surface of the silver card with a sharp pencil.

6. Firmly glue the mounted print to the larger, folded card blank. If you use a strongly contrasting color – like the maroon shown here – add a decorative border around the card with a fine silver marker pen.

PAINT STENCILS

The stencil used for this card is acetate rather than cardboard. Not only do acetate stencils last longer than those made of cardboard so you can use them time after time, but it is possible to create more complex designs with finer details. The motif used here – a crocodile – was, like the turtle card (see page 19), inspired by the art of the Australian Aborigines. The earthy colors represent the natural pigments used by native Australians, but other shades would look good. Stencil paints are available from most art shops, but they can be rather expensive. Gouache or latex paint works just as well.

see page 19

YOU WILL NEED

Acetate, 29 × 21cm
Fine felt-tipped pen
Scalpel or craft knife
Masking tape
Ingres paper: orange and
    dark brown, 20 × 9cm
Gouache paint: red, orange
Palette or saucer

Stencil brush
Colored pencils: red,
    orange, brown, yellow
Paintbrush (no. 7)
Clear, all-purpose adhesive
    or glue stick
Scissors
Cream card, 20 × 19cm

2. Use masking tape to hold the acetate stencil over the chosen paper to prevent it from slipping. Apply paint over the whole of the stencil with a stencil brush.

1. Trace the design onto a piece of acetate with a fine pen and use a scalpel or craft knife to remove the dark sections of the motif. Remove any ink that remains on the surface of the acetate with a damp tissue.

3. Remove the masking tape and carefully peel back the stencil, leaving a print of the design. Repeat the process as many times as you wish. Leave the paint to dry for 20–30 minutes.

4. Carefully tear the paper to size and use colored pencils to complete the design.

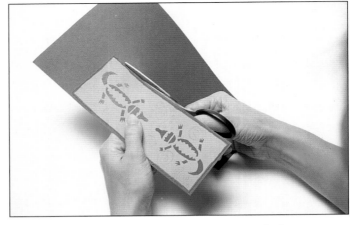

6. When the paint is dry, stick it to a background of a contrasting color. Cut it to size, leaving a narrow border of the contrasting color showing around the edge.

5. Highlight the torn edges of the paper and create a border by adding a small amount of paint to the edges with a fine paintbrush.

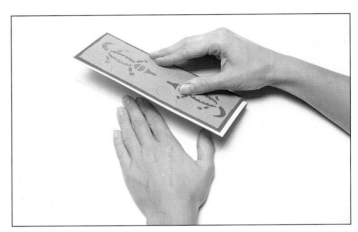

7. Fold the cream card in half and glue the finished stencil to the front of the larger piece of card.

METAL MAGIC

Rather than taking all your empty aluminum drink cans to the recycling tip, try this unique method of decorating a greeting card. Linear or punched patterns can be easily created in the soft aluminum, giving an embossed effect. It is the perfect technique for all kinds of decorations. A simple bird motif was used in this project, which was inspired by American folk art. You may want to wear gloves when you are cutting the metal because the edges are quite sharp.

YOU WILL NEED

Empty aluminum can
Metal scriber
Metal snips
Tracing paper
Fine, black felt-tipped pen
Fine wire wool
Pencil and ruler

Dark blue mounting card,
    9 × 8cm
Craft knife
White card, 20 × 15cm
Double-sided adhesive
    tape
Fine silver marker pen

1. Carefully pierce the can with a scriber to make a hole. Insert the snips into the hole and cut off the top of the can.

2. Cut down the side of the can and remove the base. Once the metal is opened out, trim off any uneven edges and cut off a section of metal to work with.

3. Transfer the image of the bird to the reverse (patterned) side of the metal. Use a felt-tipped pen rather than a ball-point pen so that you do not mark the metal. Arrange the motif so that there is at least 1.5cm all round. Go over the lines of the design with a scriber.

4. When you have completed scribing gently rub over the surface of the metal with wire wool and trim it to size if necessary. Place the metal on a piece of mounting card and draw a line around it. The card will form the mount for the metal.

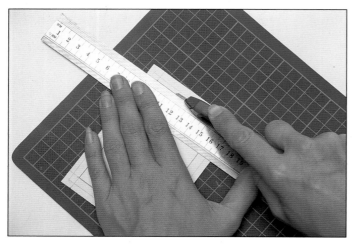

5. Measure, then draw a border on the mounting board. Draw a third line, at least 0.5cm inside the first, so that the mount will hold the metal in place.

6. Cut along the outside line on the cardboard, and then cut out the central window of the blue card.

7. Use double-sided tape to stick the metal to the front of the white card. Tape is better than adhesive because the metal has a springy quality that makes it difficult for glue to adhere to the surface.

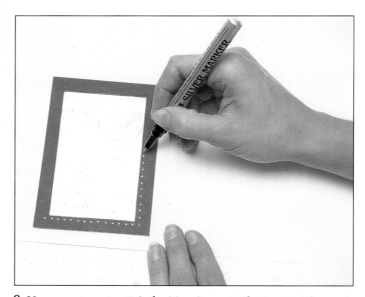

8. Use more tape to stick the blue frame to the front of the card so that the motif is centered in the window. If you wish, add small decorative dots with a silver pen.

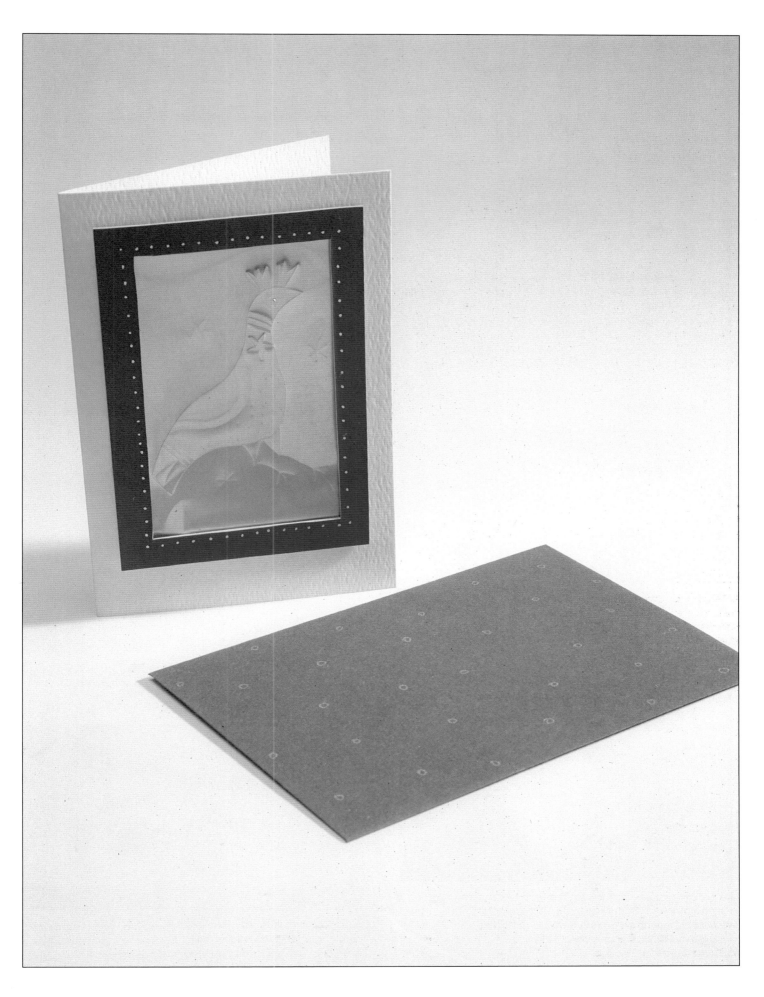

INVITATIONS AND TAKE-HOME BAGS

This bright and festive invitation would be suitable for almost any occasion, but the matching "take-home" bags are ideal for a children's party, when the guests have little presents to take home with them. The motif and decorations are created with simple rubber stamps, and although the pigment ink pad looks rather intimidating, it is easy to use and creates wonderful effects. The materials listed below are sufficient for one card and one bag.

YOU WILL NEED

2 rectangles cream card, each about 13 × 8cm
Rubber stamps: star burst, crown, frame
Symphonic pigment ink pad
Crystal embossing powder
Heat source
Deckle-edged scissors
Green card, 20 × 15cm
Red paper, 14 × 9cm

Clear, all-purpose adhesive
Sharp, pointed scissors or craft knife
Colored paper bag
Silver pigment pad
Cosmetic sponge
Self-adhesive pads or double-sided adhesive tape
Silver felt-tipped pen

---

1. Place one of the rectangles of cream card on a piece of scrap paper and, using the blue and green section of the ink pad and the star burst stamp, print around the edge of the paper so about half the image appears.

2. Using the yellow and red portion of the ink pad, print the crown in the center of the cream card. Before the paint is dry, shake some crystal embossing powder on the surface. Apply heat (a hand-held paint stripper is ideal), following the manufacturer's instructions.

3. Trim the edge of the cream card with deckle-edged scissors or tear it carefully against a metal ruler.

4. Score and fold the green card and stick the red paper to the front of it. Finish by positioning the cream card on the red paper and sticking it in place.

5. Make the bag by using the yellow and red section of the ink pad, ink the crown and print it in the center of the other rectangle of cream card.

6. Emboss the crown with crystal embossing powder. When it is cool and perfectly dry, carefully cut out the crown with sharp scissors or a craft knife and put it to one side.

8. Use a piece of cosmetic sponge to make a cloud of silver ink below the frame.

7. Ink the frame stamp with silver ink and print the image on the top section of the bag.

9. Use a self-adhesive pad or some double-sided tape to attach the crown to the bag in the center of the silver cloud. Add the recipient's name with a silver felt-tipped pen.

PENCIL PACKAGING

A large colored paper pencil is a novel way to wrap a gift. Fill the pencil with novelty items, stationery, or with sweets. If the pencil is large enough, use it for a T-shirt, scarf, or pair of gloves. Fill the end of the pencil with crumpled tissue paper and make a pencil gift tag in a contrasting color.

YOU WILL NEED

Medium weight paper:
  white, yellow, blue
Tracing paper
Ruler
Scalpel
Double-sided adhesive
  tape or clear, all-
  purpose adhesive

30

1. Cut out a rectangle of yellow paper measuring 28 × 25cm. Use the template (BELOW RIGHT) to cut out the point of the pencil from pieces of yellow and white paper.

2. Form the rectangle into a tube and stick the long sides together. Form the yellow and white points into cones, making sure that they fit inside the end of the tube. Stick the yellow cone over the white cone.

3. Make a contrasting pencil tag and thread through some plastic thread. Push the top of the pencil into the tube and hold it in place with adhesive tape.

Half size

TWIST-OUT CARDS

This is an ingenious way of creating three-dimensional cards. Use thin card – paper is too weak, and thick card is too cumbersome to bend easily. The basic method is explained here, and the technique can be easily adapted to all kinds of shapes, geometric and representational.

YOU WILL NEED

Card
Scalpel or craft knife
Scissors
Pencil and ruler

1. Draw a line (AB) down the center of a piece of card.

2. Use a blade to incise line C to D so that the incision starts and ends on AB. Note that AC is shorter than DB.

3. Next, incise line E to F so that the incision starts and ends on line AB. Note that E is below C and F is below D.

4. Pull edge GH towards you and push IJ away from you, forming short creases between CE and DF.

5. The center of the card will twist out from its frame.

BELOW: Twist-outs make highly individual greeting cards. The words and shapes can be altered to suit every occasion.

QUILLED GIFT TAGS

The technique of quilling or paper filigree involves using rolled strips of paper to form shapes, which can be glued together and stuck to a base card to make patterns. The designs can be used in various ways, but they are especially appropriate for gift tags and small cards. The strips should be about 0.3cm wide, and the length can vary. Some stationery shops sell pre-cut strips, and these are worth looking out for because cutting them by hand is extremely laborious, especially if you are planning a fairly ambitious project.

Use a cocktail stick, matchstick, or a piece of dowel with a split in the end. Place one end of the strip in the split and turn it slowly and evenly so that the strip remains level. When the paper is completely rolled, squeeze it lightly to make a tight curve before removing the stick.

You can plan patterns in advance or build them up as you go along. It is best to work on a piece of waxed paper so that you can move the designs around as your work progresses. If you are making a decoration for a card and have a good idea of the scheme, glue the center of the shape and place each part of the design carefully in position. A second cocktail stick or a pair of tweezers are useful for controlling the coils. Finished designs can be sprayed with paint or varnish.

Plain gift tags can be decorated using quilling. Use the little coils of paper to create some unusual shapes and patterns.

WHAT A CRACKER!

Most pop-up cards open with a single crease, but here, to mimic the movement of an exploding cracker, two creases are needed. To hold the design tight shut during transit, a lock must be constructed across the central opening. Note how the four pop-up elements fly off two small rectangular tabs cut from the backing sheet and off two triangles glued to it. The triangles can be cut from the backing sheet, but this will weaken the card. The grid is drawn to a scale of 1:2.

YOU WILL NEED

Backing sheet (thin red glossy card), 30 × 20cm
Adhesive tape
Blue and yellow glossy

card (for letters), 25 × 10cm in total
Blue foil on white card (for cracker), about 20 ×15cm

Scissors
Craft knife or scalpel
Clear, all-purpose adhesive

KEY

———— cut along this line

———— suggested artwork

———— mountain crease

———— valley crease

▭ glue here (sometimes on the underside)

× 2

Triangular supports

Cracker halves

× 2

Cracker explosions

× 2

× 2

Card lock

BANG

Letters

1. Use the template (ABOVE) to cut out the pieces. Incise small square tabs as shown, one on each crease of the backing sheet. Glue the triangular supports flat against the creases.

2. Make sure that the creases on the support align accurately with the creases on the triangles.

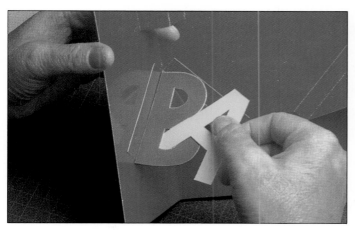

3. Glue the letters B and A to the left-hand support.

4. Glue N and G to the other support.

5. Glue one cracker half to the left-hand square tab.

6. Similarly, glue the other half to the right-hand tab. Add the explosions.

7. Close the card and add the two halves of the lock, intertwining them. When they are carefully aligned, the lock halves will hold the card tightly shut.

FOR THE UNDER-10s

*This design uses a single piece of card and a cut-away technique to make part of the pop-up –
the top half of the number – stand freely. When you are making the card, measure the
distances carefully so that the number is well proportioned and well positioned. Working out
the geometry of a single-piece pop-up card can be difficult. The simple step shape used here,
with the top half of the number lifted from the background, can be adapted for other numbers
or letters or even words and objects. The grid is drawn to a scale of 1:2½.*

YOU WILL NEED

Medium weight blue
   paper, 32 × 15cm
Scissors or scalpel
Yellow self-adhesive dots
Felt-tipped pens

KEY

— cut along this line
— suggested artwork
— mountain crease
— valley crease
— these measurements
   are the same

1. Cut along the solid lines shown on the template (LEFT).

2. Fold the two ends of the central crease.

3. Fold the bottom crease.

4. Fold along the top crease and turn the card over.

5. Fold the remaining short, central creases at each side of the number.

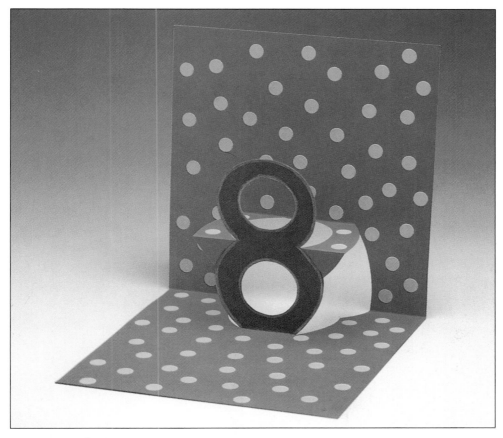

6. This is the completed pop-up shape, which will fold flat.

LIGHT THE CANDLE

One-piece pop-up cards are always satisfying to make because you can see a three-dimensional shape emerge as if by magic from what was a flat piece of card. The geometry, though, can be a little mystifying. The key is to measure the placement of all the creases carefully and to understand which distances are equal to other distances. For best results, before making a finished card, make a rough card so that you can check that you understand which measurements must be equal. The grid is drawn to a scale of 1:2½.

KEY

—— cut along this line

—— suggested artwork

—— mountain crease

—— valley crease

—— these measurements
      are the same

YOU WILL NEED

Thin cream-colored card,
  34.4 × 15cm
Ruler
Scalpel
Felt-tipped pens or
  crayons

1. Cut along the thick lines shown on the template (LEFT).

2. Fold the long bottom crease.

3. Fold the creases to each side of the candle and turn over the card carefully.

4. Fold the creases around the flame.

5. Fold the front edge of the step to complete the card.

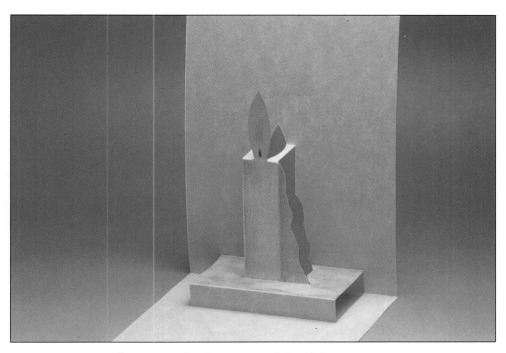

6. The completed pop-up card. Careful measuring and creasing will permit the candle to fold flat.

CLASHING COLORS

*Bright and jazzy giftwrap appeals to adults and children alike. Wrapping ordinary boxes in
wonderfully colored papers is a simple way of creating fun gift wrapping.*
*Choose a paint that contrasts with the paper. Make it quite runny, dip in an old toothbrush
and flick on to the paper. Decorate with paper ribbon and sweets.*
*Spatter a box with a clashing color of paint and make a matching tag. Wrap with paper ribbon
and add some marzipan vegetables threaded on to a wooden skewer.*

STAMPED GIFT TAGS

These simple little tags are easy to make but are a perfect way of adding a personal touch to a gift. Mulberry paper is like tissue paper, but it has a fibrous texture. It can be used to print on and emboss with powder, and it is ideal for all kinds of decorative uses. When it is torn, the edges feather prettily.

YOU WILL NEED

Maple leaf stamp
Ink pad in shades of
   green
Self-adhesive note pad
Sharp, pointed scissors
Cream paper, 8 × 4cm
Dark green mulberry
   paper

Deckle-edged scissors
Clear, all-purpose
   adhesive
Ready-made gift tag blank
   or cream card, scored
   and folded

3. When the ink on the printed leaf is dry, place the mask over it. Print a second leaf, to the right of the first one, using the medium shade of green. Clean the stamp.

1. Make a mask by stamping the maple leaf onto a sheet of the note pad – make sure that the image is positioned close to the sticky portion of the pad. Carefully cut out the image and put it to one side.

4. Still with the mask in place over the first leaf, ink the stamp with the light shade of green and print a third leaf, this time to the left of the first one. When the ink is dry, carefully remove the mask.

2. Print the leaf in the darkest shade of green on the cream paper. Clean the stamp by pressing it alternately on a damp paper towel and a dry paper towel.

5. Tear or use deckle-edged scissors to cut a piece of the mulberry paper so that it is about 0.5cm less all round than the gift tag blank.

6. Glue the mulberry paper to the front of the gift tag.

7. Carefully cut out the printed leaves and glue them to the center of the mulberry paper.

STENCIL GIFT TAGS

These little gift tags are simple to make, and they are an ideal project to introduce children to the art of stenciling. A white heart on red paper and a yellow star on green were used, but the colors can be changed to match the wrapping paper. The steps below describe how to make and use a simple stencil.

YOU WILL NEED

Colored paper, 10 × 8cm
Hole punch
Tracing paper
Acetate
Scalpel or craft knife
Stencil or acrylic paint
Saucer
Stencil brush
Curling ribbon

2. Practice by putting a small amount of red paint in a saucer or palette. Dip the brush into the paint and then rub off the excess on a paper towel so that the brush is almost dry.

1. Fold the paper in half lengthways and punch a hole in the top left-hand corner, leaving sufficient room for the design. Trace the motif of your choice, lay a piece of acetate on the tracing, and use a craft knife or scalpel to cut out the shape.

3. Place the stencil over a piece of scrap paper and hold it firmly in place with one hand. Hold the stencil brush upright and press it through the stencil cut-out, moving it with a circular motion around the inside edge of the stencil. Continue to build up color by moving the brush around the edges, but try not to let the color build up in the center of the cut-out.

4. If your brush is too wet with paint, it may result in a flat, filled-in stencil shape that bleeds around the edges (as in the top heart). The drier the brush, the better, although if it is too dry the image will be too faint (center heart). The heart at the bottom, with the shaded edges and light center area is ideal.

5. When you are confident, use the technique on the card, building up the color in a circular motion around the edge of the cut-out. Finally, twirl a length of ribbon and thread it through the hole.

BASIC BOX

When you are drawing a plan for a basic box, work out the dimensions and, whatever the size, make sure that all the angles are 90 degrees (see Fig 1). The larger the box, the thicker the card should be. The number of flaps should equal the number of edges, and all flaps should be at least 1cm deep, although if you are making a very large box, you might want to make the flaps 2cm or more.

YOU WILL NEED

Thin card
Pencil and ruler
Craft knife or scalpel
Scissors
Bone folder
Pair of compasses
Protractor and/or set
 square
Clear, all-purpose
 adhesive
Double-sided adhesive
 tape

1. Use a sharp craft knife to cut out the shape. Always cut away from your work so that you do not accidentally cut into the box side.

2. Check the fit of the box, then glue the sides together.

3. Glue the base in position.

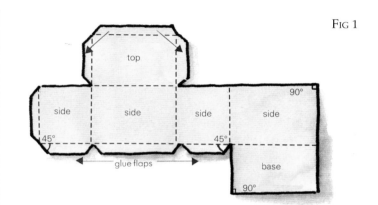

FIG 1

45

BELOW: Card can be simply decorated in dozens of ways, including collage, stenciling, and marbling, and then made into boxes to hold all manner of things. Alternatively, use plain card, and add colorful ribbons, bows, and tags, or cover plain card with shop-bought gift-wrap.

HANDMADE PAPER

Each handmade sheet of paper is unique, and it can be used to make unusual wrapping paper, boxes, cards, and envelopes. Handmade paper incorporating flowers and leaves is surprisingly easy to make. Lavender or thyme will give it an aromatic quality, and petals, ferns, and grasses can be added to give color and texture. Before you begin, you need to make a mold and deckle. The mold is a rectangular frame of wood with a fine mesh stretched across it. The deckle is an identical frame without the mesh that sits on top of the mesh side of the mold. You can buy them, but if you want to make your own, see step 1 below.

YOU WILL NEED

1.8m × 2cm wood
Saw
Waterproof adhesive
Nails
Nylon curtain mesh, 30 × 30cm
Staple gun
2 pieces of plywood, each 25 × 30cm
Shallow plastic tray
3 large sheets of newspaper

Thin, absorbent kitchen cloths
Sheets of waste paper, such as newspaper, photocopy paper, old envelopes, and so on
Electric blender
Flower petals, lavender, ferns, herbs, grasses, and so on
Plastic dish-washing bowl

1. Cut the 1.8m × 2cm wood into four pieces, each 25cm long, and four pieces, each 20cm long. Glue the pieces together to form two identical rectangles, butting the corners neatly together. When the glue is dry, nail the pieces together. Stretch the nylon mesh over one of the frames, using a staple gun to hold it taut. Trim away any excess fabric.

2. Make a couching mound to ease the transfer of the layers of paper pulp from the mold to the couching cloths. Lay a plywood rectangle in the shallow tray. Fold the newspaper into various sizes and place them on top of the plywood. Cover with a kitchen cloth and moisten with water.

3. Half fill the blender jug with water. Tear the waste paper into small pieces, about 2.5 × 2.5cm, and add about two handfuls to the blender jug. Blend for a 10–20 second burst, add the plant materials, and blend for a further 5 seconds. Pour four or five jugs of pulp into the dish-washing bowl and top up with water until the bowl is about half full.

4. Place the wooden deckle on top of the mesh side of the mold, holding both together along the shorter sides. Insert them into the pulp at an angle of about 45 degrees. Draw both up through the pulp so that the mold and deckle are horizontal.

5. Lift the mold and deckle from the water, a layer of paper pulp will have been deposited on the mesh. Hold it over the bowl for a second or two to allow the water to drain away, then remove the deckle, and place the pulp-covered mesh side of the mold on the couching mound.

6. Lift the mold, leaving the pulp layer on the mound. Cover it with another kitchen cloth, and repeat the whole process again. Build up 8–10 layers, then place the other plywood rectangle on top. Squeeze the plywood pieces together to remove excess water. Carefully peel off the kitchen cloths with the pulp layers still attached, and leave them in a warm, dry place to dry completely. The paper sheets can then be removed from the cloths.

47

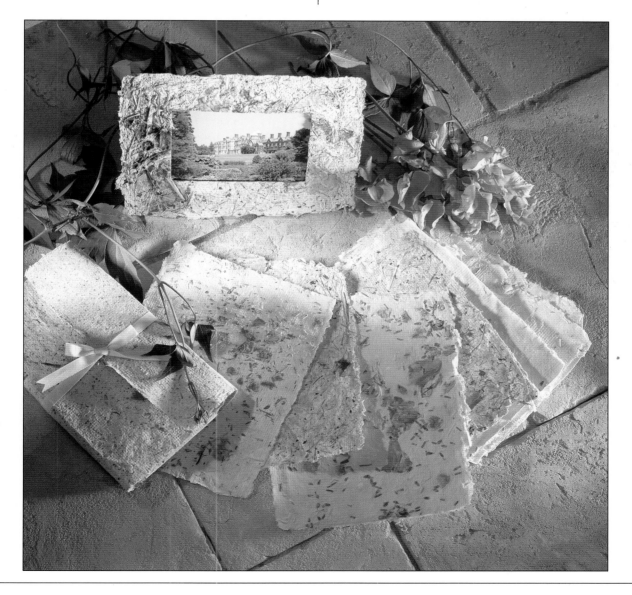

ENVELOPES

It is quite simple to make your own envelopes, and when you have taken the trouble to make a card, it seems a shame to spoil the effect by either not finding an envelope that fits or using one that does not match. A natural colored envelope was used here, and decorated simply with a few swirls, but the decoration can be as complicated or as restrained as you want.

YOU WILL NEED

Sheet of paper to match
   card, about 42 × 30cm
Pencil
Ruler
Scissors
Glue stick

48

1. Place the card for which you are making the envelope on the chosen paper. Measure around the card, allowing a border of 0.5cm on all sides. Draw in the lines.

2. Mark the center of your drawing with a cross, drawn by measuring in from the corners.

3. Measure from the center point (where the diagonals bisect) to the edge of the top and the edge of the bottom sections. Add this measurement, plus 1.5cm for the overlap, and make a mark. Draw lines from the corners to these marks to form the flaps of the envelope.

4. Repeat the process for the side flaps, but do not add the extra 2.5cm.

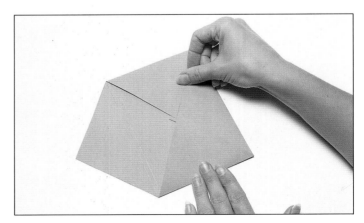

5. Cut out the finished shape then fold in the flaps at the sides to form an envelope.

6. Apply a small amount of glue to the edges of the bottom of the envelope. Fold it over and stick it down over the side flaps.

7. The envelope can then be decorated with a gold pen, as shown. Alternatively, you can use cork stamps, stencils or whatever you wish to complement the card.

CARDS FROM NATURE

A simple method of producing unique greeting cards is to collect feathers, leaves, seed pods, or dried flowers and mount them onto textured, natural-colored papers. Handmade papers are also available, many of which would complement the natural objects used.

YOU WILL NEED

A feather; chicken or duck feathers are very suitable
Sugar paper in 2 colors; pale beige and pink, 21 x 29cm
Natural color blank card, 15 x 20cm

Scissors
Craft knife
Masking tape
Cutting mat

3. Slide the shaft of the feather through the slits until the feather lies in the desired position on the paper.

1. Select your feather and its background paper. Carefully tear the paper to the correct size. A torn edge will give a more interesting effect.

4. Turn over the paper and keeping the feather in position put a piece of tape over the openings and the feather shaft to secure the feather in place. If decorating with dried leaves, seed pods etc, mount them using PVA glue and leave to dry for 30–40 minutes.

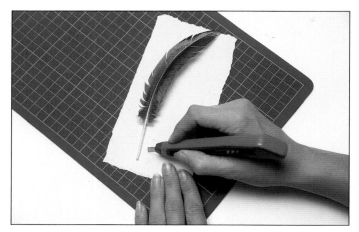

2. Place the backing paper on the cutting mat and with a craft knife, make two slits in the paper.

5. To further decorate the card, select a complementary colored paper for a background. Crumple this sheet of paper in your hands.

6. Flatten out the paper, then tear it to size. Apply glue, then stick this to a larger folded, contrasting card.

7. To complete the greeting card, glue the paper holding the feather onto the middle of the crumpled effect background.

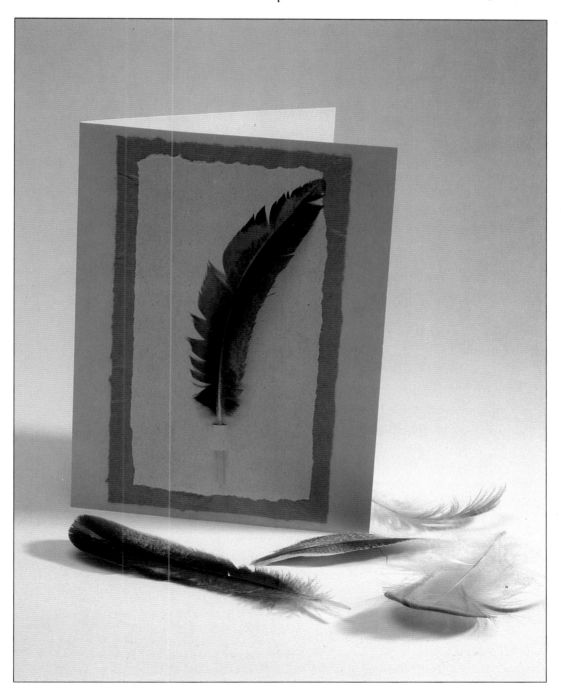

SIMPLE BAG

Bags like this are easy to make, and once you have mastered the technique they can be used in all kinds of ways. Small bags can be made with ordinary gift-wrapping paper, although if you want to make a larger bag you will need to use thicker, stronger paper. You can, for example, use ordinary brown wrapping paper and decorate it before assembling the bag. Remember that all the angles must be perfect right angles so that the bag will stand square and the bottom flaps should be about 1.5cm less than the width of the sides. If you are using thick paper or card, score the fold lines to give crisp, neat creases.

1. It is easiest to work on the wrong side of the paper. Decide on the size of the bag and draw the plan. Cut out the shape and remove the shaded areas. Score the dotted lines lightly, and fold and unfold them.

2. Glue down the top flap, which adds strength and looks neater. Next glue the front flap to the side.

3. Finally, glue the bottom flaps to each other – the side flaps to the back flap and the front flap on top of the side flaps.

STRONG PAPER BAG

If you are going to make a bag to contain a heavy gift, such as a bottle, glue a piece of card inside the base of the bag. To strengthen the top, add an extra strip of paper under the top flap. The basic plan is the same as for a simple bag, except that the measurements for all sides should be identical and should be the diameter of the bottle, plus 0.5cm. The height of the bag should be 6cm more than the height of the bottle so that the top edges can be drawn together.

1. It is possible to fold the bag flat by scoring lines in addition to the ones on the basic plan. Practice with some scrap paper – it is not as complicated as it looks.

2. When you are making a large bag, add a strong handle by cutting a piece of plain, lightweight card the width of the bag and at least 7.5cm deep. Cut the hand shape out of the center of the card and mark this hole on the bag plan. Cut these holes out of the paper on the bag and top flap, and glue the card stiffener in position before proceeding as for the basic bag.

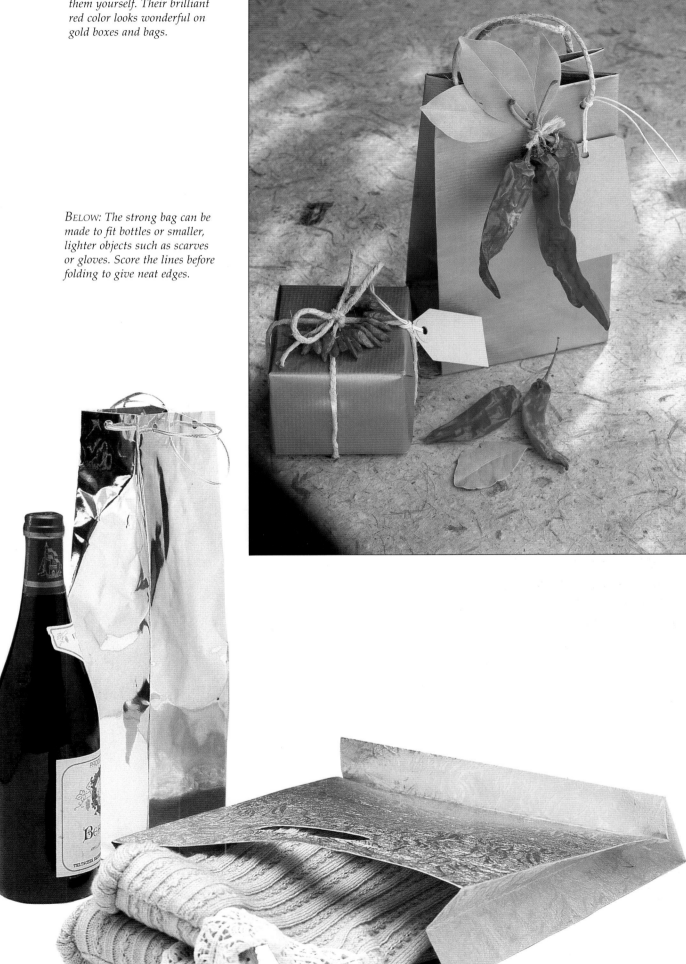

RIGHT: You can buy chiles ready dried or you can dry them yourself. Their brilliant red color looks wonderful on gold boxes and bags.

BELOW: The strong bag can be made to fit bottles or smaller, lighter objects such as scarves or gloves. Score the lines before folding to give neat edges.

GIFT BAGS

These charming little country-look bags take the idea of using bags for awkwardly shaped gifts a stage further – they are perfect for even the most bizarre shapes. Enlarge the size of the template on a photocopier if you want to make a larger bag.

YOU WILL NEED

Tracing paper
White card for template
Ruler and pencil
Check cotton fabric
Paper or card with a
  textured surface
Knife
Scissors
PVA adhesive

Paintbrush
Double-sided adhesive
  tape
Leather punch
Fine string
Small buttons with two
  holes
Thin colored card

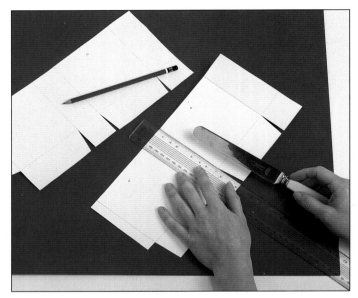

2. To make the fabric-covered bag, cut a piece of cloth about 2.5cm larger all round than the template. Glue the card shape to the fabric, carefully smoothing out any wrinkles and bubbles. Trim the fabric close to the card, leaving 2.5cm excess at the upper edge. Crease at the fold positions again.

1. Trace the template (page 56) and transfer all the fold lines accurately. The template shows both sizes. For the bag made of card, cut out a box shape in colored or textured card. For the fabric-covered bag, use thin white card. Score along all dotted lines.

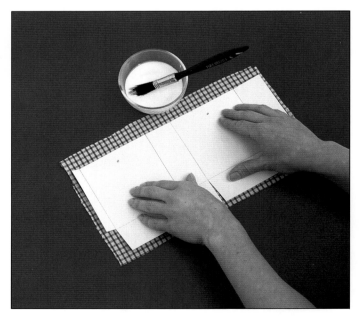

3. Use double-sided tape to hold the tab to the side edge.

4. Fold in the flaps at the lower edge to form the bottom of the bag. Hold the flaps in place with double-sided tape.

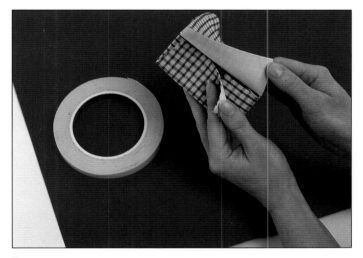

5. If you are making the fabric-covered bag, apply a strip of double-sided tape to the inside of the top edge. Turn the fabric down neatly all round.

6. Make a fastening by using the leather punch to pierce a hole in the center of the bag, about 2cm down from the top edge.

7. Cut a piece of string about 25cm long for each bag. Fold the string in half, then thread the ends through the holes in the button and tie a knot. Next, thread the loop end through the punched holes at the top of the bag, then bring the loop around the button at the front. This makes a pretty and secure fastening.

8. To make the fish gift tag, trace the template (page 56). Cut one shape from thin, colored card. Score and fold it along the dotted line. Pierce a small hole at the head end, using a paper punch. Glue on a small button for the eye. Knot a short length of string and tie up the bag with a neat bow.

Tab

Fold

Gift Bag Heart Motif

Gift Bag Fish Tag

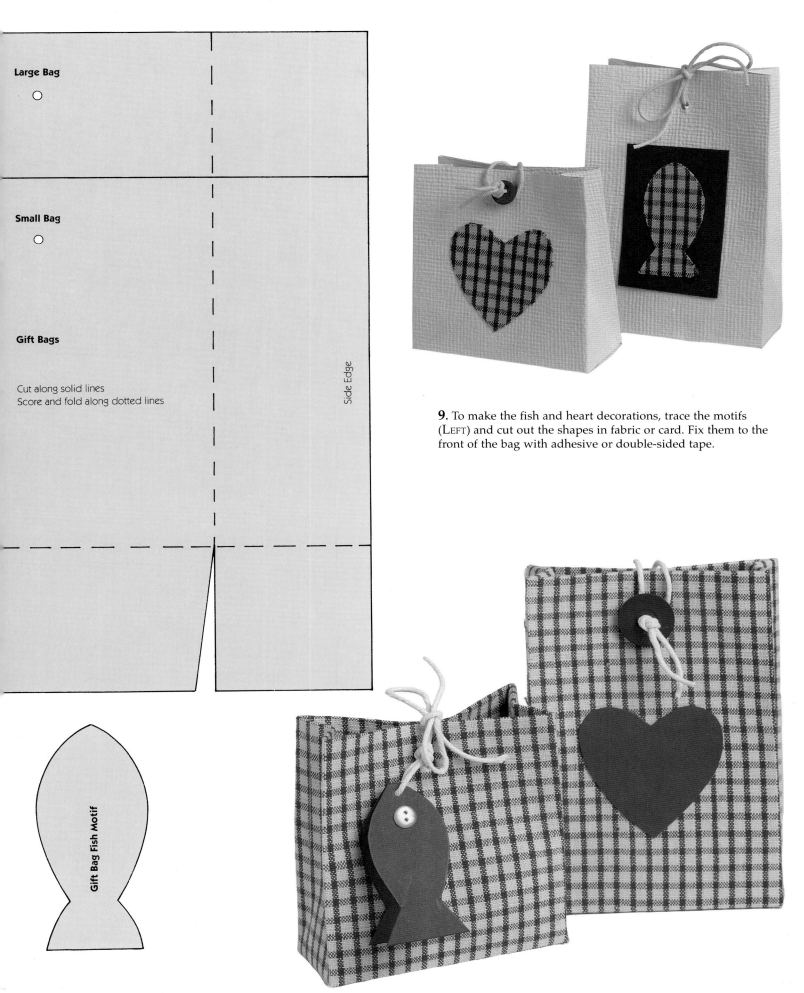

Large Bag

Small Bag

Gift Bags

Cut along solid lines
Score and fold along dotted lines

Side Edge

Gift Bag Fish Motif

9. To make the fish and heart decorations, trace the motifs (LEFT) and cut out the shapes in fabric or card. Fix them to the front of the bag with adhesive or double-sided tape.

SPECIAL OCCASIONS

One of the secrets of success is to coordinate all the elements of your gifts – wrapping paper, ribbon, tag, and card. Even if you use shop-bought paper try to make each gift special by adding your own decoration to the shop-bought elements. Presents for special occasions require a little thought. Wedding gifts are often wrapped in white, with silver decorations. Look out for metallic and voile ribbons and for silk flowers, which can be added to a plainly wrapped parcel to make a pretty bouquet.

It is, however, sometimes more fun to try something a little unusual. Crepe papers are available in some rich, vibrant colors, and you can sometimes find these papers with a contrasting color on the reverse, which are especially useful for simple tags. Cover boxes with brightly colored crepe paper, then cut a strip of a contrasting color, long enough to go around the box. Slightly stretch this strip to give it a wavy, crinkled edge, and then wrap this band around the center of the parcel before decorating with colored paper flowers.

WEDDING INVITATION

This elegant design would be perfect for a wedding invitation, but the card would be just as suitable for Mother's Day or for sending someone Easter greetings. The pattern is made from a rubber stamp, but the finished card requires the use of several techniques to give this lovely effect of stained glass. You will need to heat the embossing powder – a hand-held paint stripper is ideal – but take care that it does not become too hot.

YOU WILL NEED

Oval floral frame rubber
  stamp
Embossing ink
Tracing paper, 13 × 8cm
Gold embossing powder
Heat source
Watercolor paints
Paintbrush

White card, 28 × 10cm
Yellow mulberry paper,
  14 × 9.5cm
Clear, all-purpose adhesive
Cream card, 13 × 8cm
Deckle-edged scissors

2. Place the tracing paper face down on a piece of light colored scrap paper, and use watercolor paints to color in the design from the back.

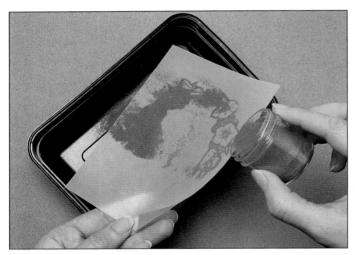

1. Use the embossing ink to print the floral frame stamp onto the tracing paper. Before the ink is dry, sprinkle over the gold embossing powder, tap off the excess and apply heat to emboss the powder.

3. Score and fold the white card. Open it out and position the yellow mulberry paper on the front half. Glue in place.

4. Trim the cream card with the deckle-edged scissors. Do not cut too much off – there should be an even border of yellow showing all around when you glue the cream card into place on the mulberry paper.

5. Trim the tracing paper with deckle-edged scissors so that it is the same size as the cream card. Carefully glue it to the card.

FABRIC-TRIMMED CARDS

Fabric braids and trimmings make it possible to create some unusually textured cards. You do not have to buy special lengths, although it is worth looking out for unusual braids for particular occasions. Rich reds and golds have been used here, which makes the cards suitable for a wedding anniversary, especially when they are used on deep red card.

YOU WILL NEED

Different types of braids
PVA adhesive or double-
  sided adhesive tape
Old paintbrush
Fabric cutting scissors
Dark red card, 15 × 10cm

62

1. Choose the different braids and cut them to size.

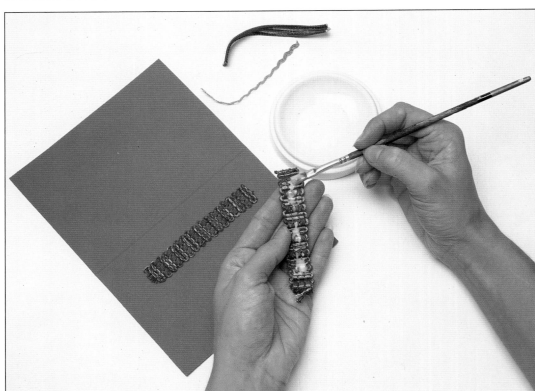

2. Arrange the braids on the cards and stick them down. You can apply adhesive directly to the back of the braid or, if you prefer, use double-sided adhesive tape.

3. Build up layers of different colors and textures. If you have used adhesive, leave it to dry for about 1 hour.

PRESENTATION ENVELOPE

How a card is presented is often as important as the card itself. Simply handing the card over in a plain envelope can seem a little thoughtless, especially if the occasion is an important one. So here is an attractive and versatile way to make a presentation envelope. Note how the lock is symmetrical, no matter which edge is folded first.

YOU WILL NEED

Sheet of stiff paper
Pencil
Ruler
Pair of compasses

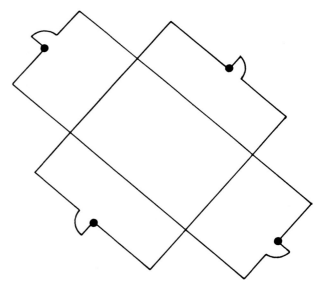

1. In the middle of a piece of stiff paper, draw a line around the card, a little distance away from it, to compensate for the card's thickness.

2. Remove the card and extend the horizontal and vertical lines on the inside of the card. Draw the diagonals to locate the center.

3. Measure the distances from the center point to the edges of the card outline.

4. Reproduce these distances beyond the central rectangle. Mark the four points with dots. The location of the four outer dots is critical. From this point on, the shapes of the locking flaps can be altered – this is just one way.

5. Draw rectangles passing through the outer dots. Keep the edges parallel and the corners square.

6. Use a pair of compasses to draw the shapes of four quarter circles so that they protrude from the four rectangular flaps. Note that the center of each quarter circle is one of the dots located in step 4 and that they lie to the right of the dot, working clockwise. Cut out the complete shape.

7. Fold in one edge.

8. Fold in the next edge, working anticlockwise.

9. Fold in the third edge, tucking it under the quarter circle opposite the first edge.

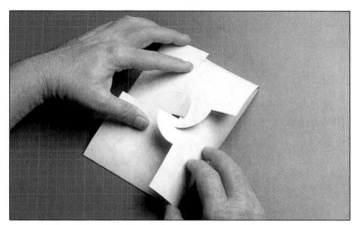

10. Fold in the fourth edge, folding it over the third and under the first.

STAMPED HEARTS

It is possible to make stamping tools from a variety of materials, including card, potato, and sponge. For this card corks were used, which, unlike potatoes, do not deteriorate over time, so you can use and reuse them whenever you want. This particular design is for a wedding card. The stamped patterns form a circle that is symbolic of fidelity and perpetual renewal. You could incorporate names or dates into the design or even paste a small photograph into the center of the circle.

YOU WILL NEED

2 corks from wine bottles
Fine marker pen
Craft knife or scalpel
Pair of compasses
White crayon
Blue sugar paper, about
   15 × 10cm

Palette or saucer
Gouache paint: white
Silver ink
Silver pen
White card, about
   31 × 21cm

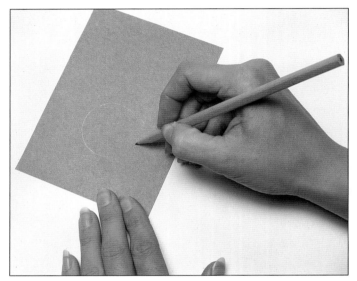

2. Use compasses or a small jar to draw a circle on the paper you intend to print on. The circle is a guide for positioning the printed shapes, so do not press on heavily.

1. Draw your chosen motif on the corks and use a scalpel or craft knife to remove the areas surrounding the motifs. Do this carefully so that the edge of the pattern stands proud of the top of the corks.

3. Place some white paint and some silver ink on a palette or on a saucer. Dip one of the cork stamps into the paint and the other in the ink, and carefully apply the stamps around the circle, alternating the patterns. When you have completed the circle of stamps, leave the paint to dry for about 10 minutes.

4. Add any further details to the pattern with a silver pen before sticking the pattern to the front of a folded, contrasting piece of card.

WEDDING BELLS

This design is made from more than one piece of card, which allows greater freedom in the design – and it means that it does not have to be as precisely cut as some pop-up designs. The grid is drawn to a scale of 1:2.

YOU WILL NEED

Backing sheet (thick green reflecting foil card), 32 × 19cm
Adhesive tape
Thick green reflective card (for supports), about 15 × 15cm

Thin silver card (for bell), about 18 × 15cm
Scissors
Craft knife or scalpel
Clear, all-purpose adhesive

68

× 2

× 2

KEY

———— cut along this line

———— mountain crease

———— valley crease

▭ glue here (sometimes on the underside)

1. Cut the backing sheet in half, place it face down, butt the cut edges together, and stick them together with tape so that it will lie flat after being folded. Use the template (LEFT) to cut out the pieces. Apply glue to the tabs at each end of the support.

2. Fix the support to the backing sheet.

3. Glue the other support to the backing sheet, but reversing the tabs.

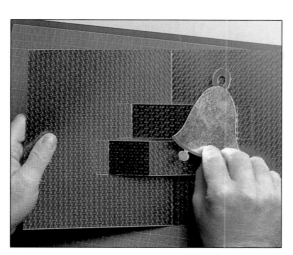

4. Glue a bell to one of the supports.

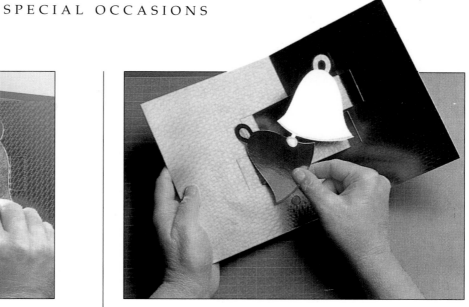

5. Glue the other bell to the other support.

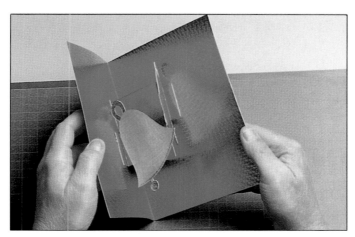

6. The card will close easily if the supports have been accurately positioned.

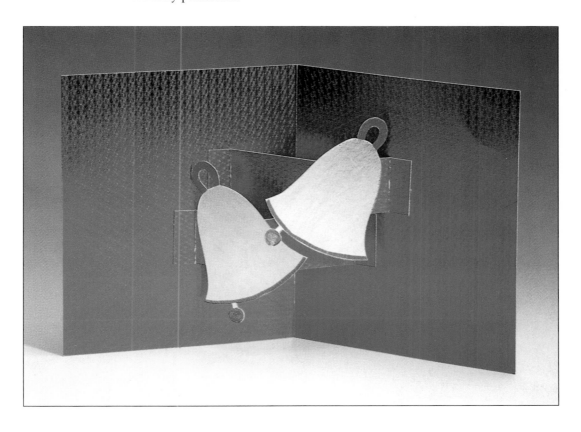

HINGED SHELL GIFT BOX

Natural shells can be hinged together to make enchanting gift boxes, particularly for small items of jewelry.

YOU WILL NEED

Large scallop shell or
  lucina shell
Sheet of medium-grade
  sandpaper

PVA glue
Small brass hinge

70

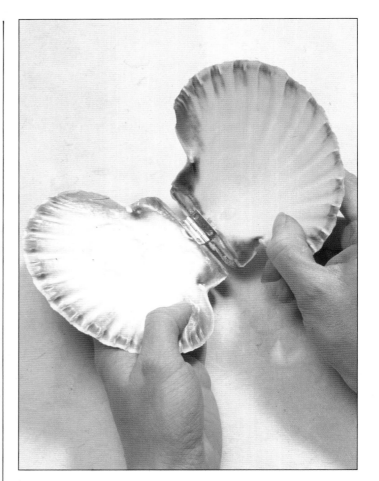

1. Wash and dry the shell carefully. Place the two halves together to give you an indication to where the hinge should be positioned. Rub the surface of the shell at the hinge position with sandpaper. This will smooth the area and provide a good surface for the glue to adhere to.

2. Glue one side of the hinge into position and allow the glue to set firmly. Glue the other side in place. Allow the glue to set completely before flexing the hinge.

WEDDING GIFTS

A home made cracker makes a very special gift. The method is shown on page 118. Choose the materials and colors to reflect the occasion – in this case pastel and white papers. The traditional wedding almonds are tied in white net and placed on decorated crepe paper.

ROSE PETAL CONFETTI

What could be more romantic – and ecologically sound – than to use real rose petals for confetti? Their random sizes, lovely soft colors, and delicate perfume take them into a different league from the more usual paper variety, and they will be the perfect finishing touch for a special day. The rose petals were dried in silica gel, so that they did not lose their color, shape, and perfume. Pack the confetti into pretty handmade boxes, tied with ribbon, raffia, or colored string. These little boxes would also be perfect for holding little gifts – candies or homemade pot pourri, for example. Just change the color scheme to suit the occasion.

YOU WILL NEED

About two full-blown roses for each box	Sharp scissors
Silica gel crystals	Double-sided adhesive tape
Small ovenproof dish	Paper punch
Spoon	Small piece of thin card
Large sheet of petal paper (available commercially)	Tracing paper
	About 30cm narrow ribbon

2. Place the dish in the oven at its lowest possible setting and leave for about 20 minutes. Check at intervals. When the petals are dry the crystals will have turned white. Remove the dish from the oven and leave to cool. Take the petals from the dish – be careful because they will be fragile – gently tapping excess powder from the petals. You may find that a soft paintbrush is helpful for brushing away any crystals that cling.

1. Carefully remove the petals from the rose. Sprinkle a layer of silica gel crystals into the base of an ovenproof dish. Add a layer of rose petals and spoon over more crystals. Continue to add layers of petals and crystals until the dish is full and the petals are completely covered.

3. Cut a rectangle measuring 30 × 20cm from the large sheet of paper. Fold the short edges of the rectangle towards the center, and overlap by 1.5cm. Hold the overlap in place with double-sided adhesive tape.

4. Use the paper punch to make two holes at the top opening for the ribbon bow.

5. Using the outline (BELOW LEFT), copy and transfer the outline of the base of the box to the thin card and cut out the shape. Score and fold the dotted lines. Use double-sided tape to hold the base in position. Fill the box with the rose petals, then thread the ribbon through the punched holes and tie with a bow.

fold

fold

Large box base template

9cm

9cm

Enlarge templates on a photocopier by 25%

fold

Small box template

13cm

fold

fold

17cm

SMALL BOX

Cut out the shape of the box from petal paper, using the template on page 74. Score along the dotted lines. Fold the sides inward so that they overlap at the center, and hold them in place with double-sided tape. Use a paper punch to make a hole at the center of the top edge. Fold the curved semicircular sections to form the bottom, and hold them together with a small piece of double-sided tape. Fill with rose petals, and tie with a ribbon bow.

PERFECT PAPER

Paper is a very versatile medium. You can create wonderful three-dimensional and textured effects with simple techniques. Both children and adults will enjoy cutting and folding, creasing and curling, and pleating papers to create original and inexpensive gift wrappings for special occasions. You will need some fine to medium weight papers in a range of colors, scissors or a scalpel, a cutting mat, and clear, all-purpose adhesive or double-sided tape.

A simple cut-out pattern of little regularly spaced squares, cut on three sides, gives an interesting effect for little effort. Lightly draw a grid on the reverse of the paper, and carefully cut the squares, making sure that the cut lines do not run into each other.

A more complicated effect can be achieved by marking a diagonal grid on the reverse of the paper. If you cut the diagonals of the squares, rather than the outlines of the squares, you can achieve a rather mysterious effect.

LEFT: Lightly fold plain paper around the box. Lay it flat again, and mark out the circular pattern on two of the box sides only. Cut out the pattern with a scalpel. Wrap the box and decorate with shredded paper and a gift tag decorated in the same way.

A small gift can look effective by cutting a pattern in only part of the paper. Add a similarly decorated tag and matching corkscrews of paper. A colored box showing through the cut paper creates an interesting effect.

78

Continue the white paper theme with a card made by folding some handmade or embossed paper in half. Cut a "vase" from plain white paper, and cut some rows of small Vs across the top. Glue the side of the vase to the card, then cut some flower and leaf shapes from white paper and glue them to the card so that they seem to be growing inside the vase.

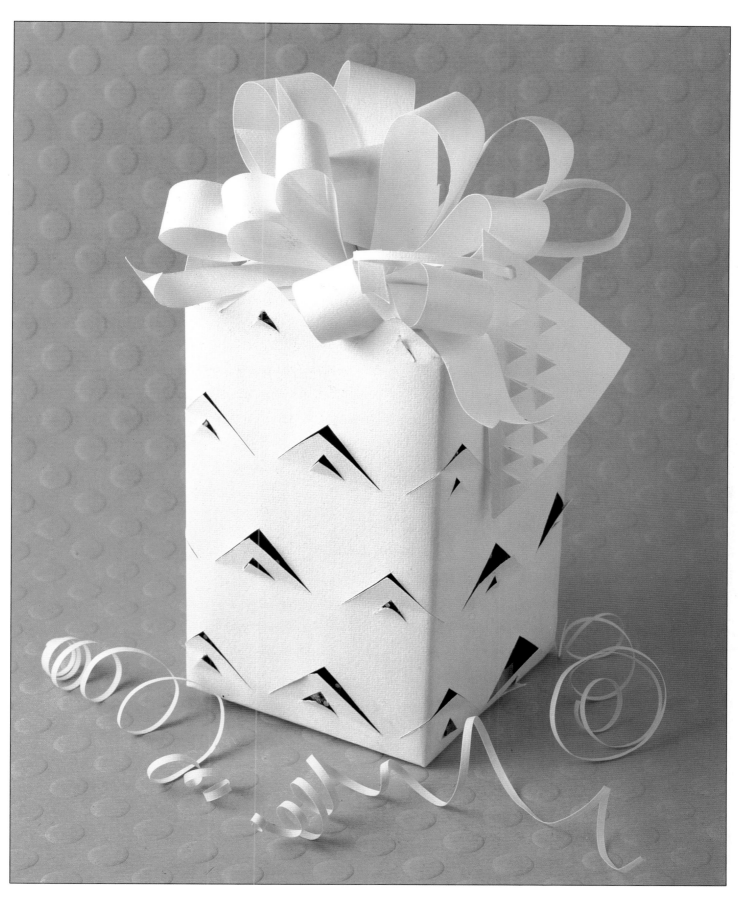

A pretty wrapping for a wedding present could be made from medium weight white paper. Make a repeating pattern of triangles, but cut only the sloping sides, not the base. Finish off with a decorative bow made by folding strips of white paper and gluing them to the top of the present. When you are cutting out these paper patterns you must use a sharp blade so that every line is clean and sharp. Use the point of a scalpel to lift the points of the triangles away from the backing.

CHRISTMAS AND
NEW YEAR

In spite of the ever-increasing range of colorful and well-designed cards and wrapping papers that are available, there is still nothing to equal the homemade version. A Christmas card is always appreciated even more when it has been made by hand, and imaginative gift wraps make any gift, no matter how small, more special. In the following section are dozens of ideas for adding a personal style to cards and parcels. They range from quick, simple ideas to more complicated projects for the special people on your Christmas list. Children can make and help with many of the ideas, and will enjoy the sponging, spattering, or potato printing.

There is, in addition, an enormous range of ribbons and papers available, and you will also find plenty of ideas for using them in unusual and intriguing ways. Remember, too, that a gift can be wrapped in fabric to make a change from paper-wrapped presents. Tartan fabrics have wonderfully rich colors and textures, and you can complement the natural look by adding bows of cotton braids and ribbon in dark, warm colors. Fresh berries, nuts, and pine cones are wonderful accompaniments. Keep a look out for remnants of fabrics in haberdashery shops, because these are often large enough for a parcel but much less expensive than specially bought lengths. Keep all your odd scraps of fabric, because you can always use them to make small bags for dried lavender or soap or to tie into bows.

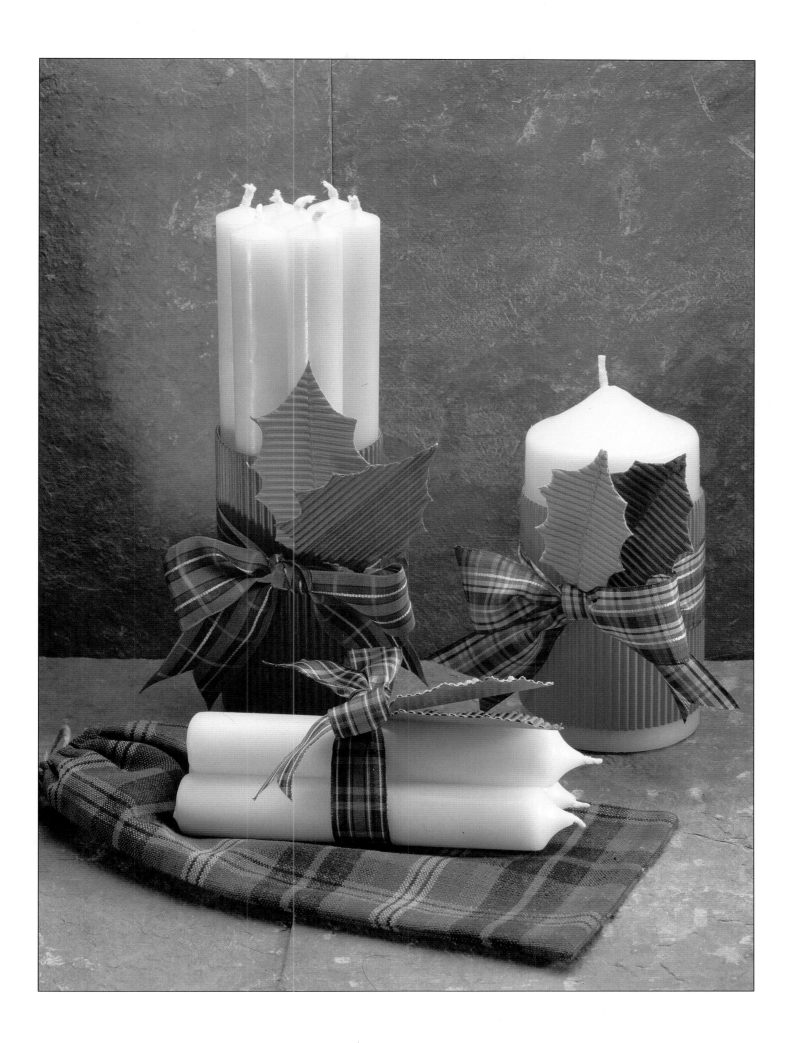

POTATO PRINTS

One of the advantages of potato prints is that it is possible to make several cards from one potato. The technique could hardly be simpler or less expensive, and it is suitable for children, although they may need help cutting the shape in the potato. Choose simple, bold motifs – potato prints are not going to give you wonderfully subtle images! Use textured paper or create an interesting base paper by spattering paint finely over the paper before you apply the potato motifs. Any thickness of paper can be used, but tissue paper works surprisingly well.

YOU WILL NEED

Colored card, 20 × 10cm
Thin card for templates
Scissors
Pencil or fine pen

Large potato
Sharp kitchen knife
Gouache or poster paints
Saucer or palette

---

1. Fold the card in half. Draw on a piece of spare card the outline of a star, Christmas tree, bell, or holly leaf, and cut around the outline to make a template.

2. Cut a large potato in half and press it against a paper towel to remove some of the moisture.

3. Use a pencil or fine marker pen to draw around your card template to transfer the image to the surface of the potato.

4. With a small kitchen knife, carefully cut around the shape. Take care that you do not mark or damage the surface of the image.

5. Dilute some gouache or poster paint in a saucer or palette and dip the surface of the potato into the paint. Press the potato firmly down on a piece of scrap paper.

6. If the shape is not fully printed, dry the paint off and carefully slice off part of the image to give a flatter surface.

7. Use the potato to print as many cards as you like. We added a border of printed strips by cutting a long, thin piece of potato so that the border had the same kind of surface texture as the printed image.

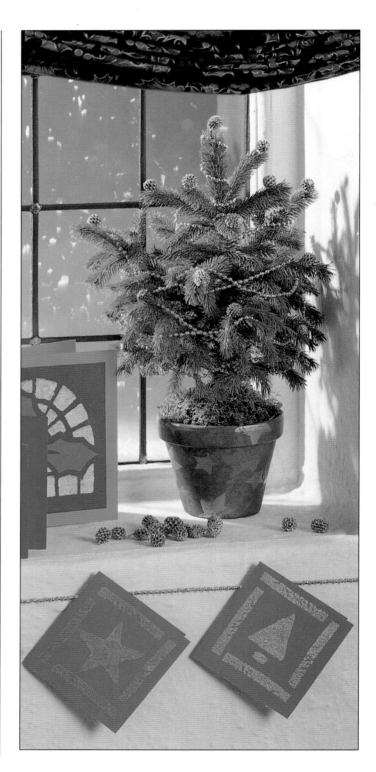

COLLAGE STAR

A creative painting technique is used to produce richly colored backgrounds on which to build layers of different papers. The end result is an unusual and individual greeting card. Collect foil paper, Christmas wrapping paper, and metallic papers for this project, and choose your paints to complement the foil. The paints used are rich purple and turquoise, and the gold star helps to create an unusual but attractive Christmas card.

YOU WILL NEED

Household sponge
Gouache paint: turquoise,
   ultramarine, purple
Palette or saucer
Garden water spray
Watercolor paper
   29 × 21cm
Gold ink
Paintbrush

Foil papers: various colors
Scissors
Clear, all-purpose adhesive
Gold card
Ruler and pencil
White card, about
   30 × 20cm
Gold pen

83

2. Select your paint colors and place them on a palette or saucer. Mist the piece of watercolor paper with water, then apply the paint to the paper using pieces of sponge.

1. Tear a household sponge into small pieces so that you can use a separate piece for each color.

3. Mist the painted surface with water again, and use a clean piece of sponge to blend the colors together.

4. Load a paintbrush with gold ink and tap it over the surface of the paint to give a stippled effect. Leave to dry for 20–30 minutes.

84

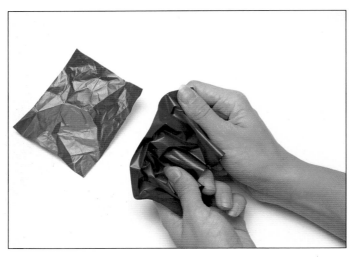

5. Select different colors of foil papers, cut them to the size you want and crumple them in your hands.

6. Glue the layers together. The largest piece, part of the painted paper, which has been torn to size, goes at the bottom, with the foil papers next, and a smaller piece, torn from the painted paper, on top.

7. Draw a small star on a piece of gold card, cut it out and stick it to the center of the collage.

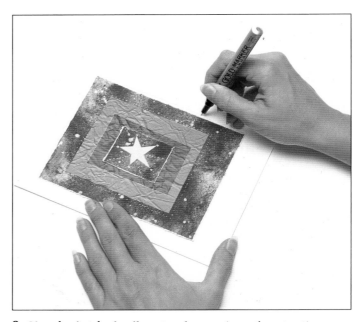

8. Glue the finished collage to a larger piece of contrasting card. Fold the card so that the collage is on the front, then draw a gold border with a fine pen to finish the design.

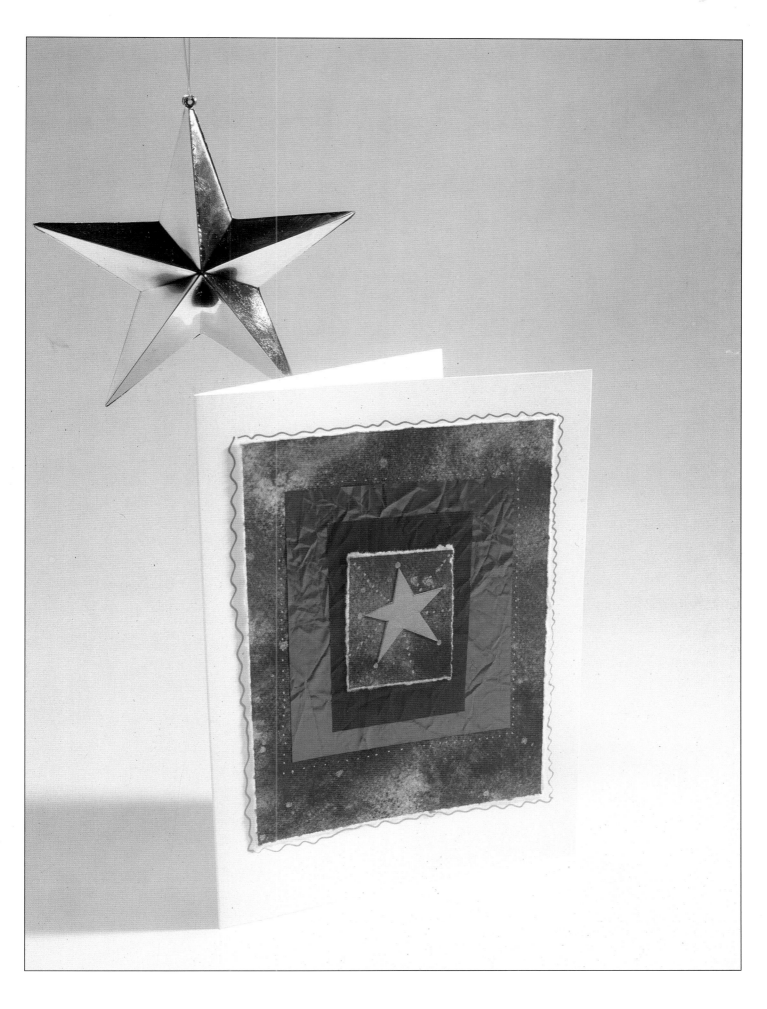

STENCILED CHRISTMAS TREE

This is a quick and easy card to make, but the technique can be adapted to make more complicated images. You can, for example, spray the stencil several times to give an overlaid effect, or you could cut several stencils and combine them to create patterns and pictures. Remember to work in a well-ventilated room when you use spray paints — better still, work outdoors if possible.

YOU WILL NEED

Stiff card for stencil,   Red cartridge paper
  12 × 9cm   Gold spray paint
Tracing paper   Fine gold marker pen
Ruler and pencil   Clear, all-purpose adhesive
Craft knife   Dark green card, 15 × 10cm

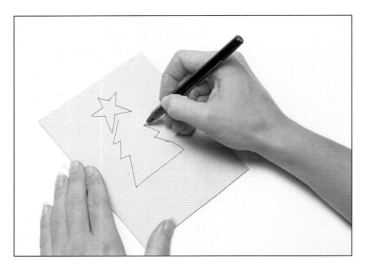

1. Draw the Christmas tree motif on the stiff card, making sure that there is at least 2cm all around the design.

3. To protect the surroundings, make a "spray booth" from a cardboard box. Place the stencil over the cartridge paper and spray over the stencil with gold paint.

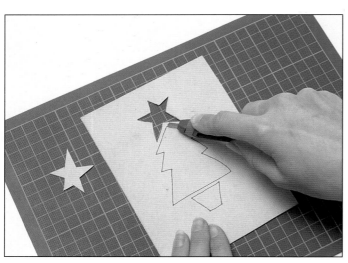

2. Use a craft knife to cut out the motifs. Rest your work on a special cutting mat or thick card to protect your work surface.

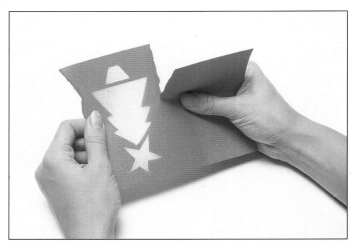

4. Allow the paint to dry (about 5 minutes) before tearing the paper to size.

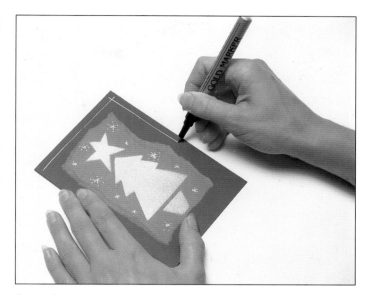

5. Add further decorative elements with a gold pen. Take the piece of paper and glue it to the front of the card.

6. Finish off by drawing in a gold border.

STENCILED WREATH

The two-part stencil used on this card was a ready-made wreath of holly leaves, which is perfect for a delicate Christmas card. Most craft shops stock a range of stencils, many made of waxed card or even thin metal, but before you buy, make sure that the pattern will be suitable for the card you want to make. On well-made two-part stencils, the first image is cut out and the complete second image is drawn in with dotted lines. The dotted lines are invaluable when you come to line up the second image.

YOU WILL NEED

Plain blank cards, white
Ready-made wreath
   stencil
Saucers or palettes

Stencil or acrylic paint:
   red, green
Stencil brushes

88

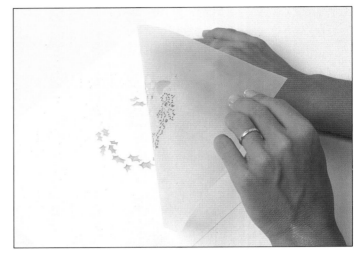

3. Hold the stencil in place but lift up a corner and look at your efforts. If the image is not strong enough, replace the stencil and continue to build up the color.

1. Separate the two parts of the stencil and put small amounts of red and green paint in different saucers.

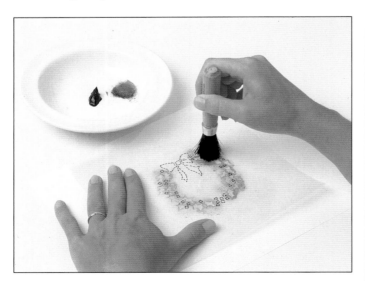

2. Place the first stencil in position over the card and dip your brush in the green paint. Blot it on a paper towel to make sure that it is not too wet, then move it confidently around the cut-out several times, working in the same direction.

4. When you are satisfied with the green, remove the stencil and leave the paint to dry completely before placing the second stencil over the first image. The bow and berries of the wreath are cut out of this stencil, but the leaves are shown as dotted lines so that you can align it accurately. Stencil the second image.

5. If you are making several cards, it is a sensible idea to stencil all the green sections first.

6. When the green paint is dry, add the red part of the pattern to all the cards. You could also add a detail of the design to the envelopes.

STAMPED CHRISTMAS TREE

Printing stamps can be used either with an ink pad or by using water-based, felt-tipped pens, which are applied directly to the stamp. We have decorated this simple Christmas tree in both ways to show how easy it is. Although we used a fairly large stamp – the image is about 13cm high – a smaller version of this would be ideal for making gift tags.

YOU WILL NEED

Rubber stamp
Ink pad or range of
 water-based felt-
 tipped pens
Cream card, about 20 ×
 15cm
Felt-tipped pens,
 watercolor paints, or
 crayons
Glitter glue or clear
 adhesive and loose
 glitter

USING AN INK PAD

1. Ink the stamp, checking that it is fully covered before printing. When you are using a larger stamp such as this tree, it is often easier to apply the pad to the stamp, rather than vice versa, because this helps to avoid the ink overflowing, especially if you are using pigment inks.

2. Print the stamp by placing it straight down on the card. Apply the necessary pressure – a delicate pattern will require little pressure, but a bolder design will need to be pressed down quite firmly. Avoid rocking the stamp from side to side, because this will blur the finished image.

3. Remove the stamp by lifting it straight up.

DECORATING THE CARD

1. Once the stamp has been printed, additional color can be added to finish the decoration. You can use felt-tipped pens, watercolor paints, or even ordinary colored crayons.

91

USING FELT-TIPPED PENS

1. Use a felt-tipped pen to apply color directly to the stamp. An advantage of using felt-tipped pens is that you can use several colors at any one time. You must work quickly, however, so that the ink does not dry.

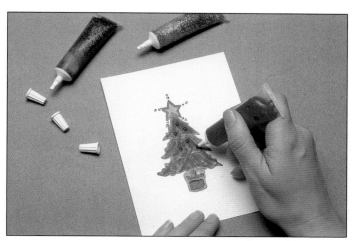

2. Glitter glue can be applied straight from the tube to add sparkling effects to the tree – we used red for the baubles and gold to add highlights to the star.

2. Before printing the stamp, moisten any dried ink by "huffing" on the image. Print in the normal way.

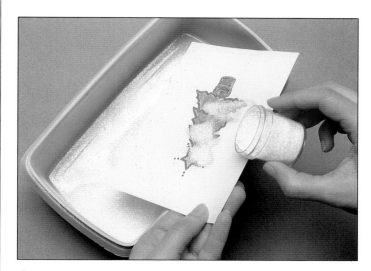

3. Alternatively, apply a few spots of adhesive and, before the glue begins to set, scatter loose glitter over the card, shaking off the excess into a tray or onto a large sheet of paper so that you can return it to the container.

POINSETTIA WREATH CARD

This pretty card is made by using a simple rubber stamp and by the additional techniques of embossing and hand coloring with felt-tipped pens.

YOU WILL NEED

Embossing pad
Poinsettia wreath rubber
  stamp
Cream card, 14 × 10cm
Black embossing powder
Heat source
Felt-tipped pens: red,

bright green, dark green
Embossing ink
Fine paintbrush
Turquoise card, about
  26 × 16cm
Clear embossing powder

92

1. Ink the stamp with the embossing ink and print the image onto the piece of cream card.

2. Before the ink dries, pour over the black embossing powder. Tap off any excess powder into a bowl.

3. Use a hand-held paint stripper to heat the embossing powder. Take care that it does not become too hot.

4. Color in the embossed design with felt-tipped pens.

5. Use a fine paintbrush to paint a thin coat of embossing ink over the colored areas.

6. Sprinkle clear embossing powder over the surface of the inked area, tap off any excess, and heat carefully. Finish the card by positioning the cream card in the center of the scored and folded turquoise card.

CANNED CHRISTMAS CARDS

These unusual cards are made from pieces of old tin cans. They are fun and easy to make, but take care when you are cutting and working with metal, and always wear protective gloves because the edges can be sharp. When you are punching out the designs, use a thick piece of card to protect your work surface. The metal we used came from the side of a large, empty coffee can. Use tin-snips to remove the bottom and top of the can, then cut down the side and open it out to form a flat sheet.

YOU WILL NEED

Tracing paper
Pencil
Ruler
Scalpel or craft knife
Colored card, some with textured surface
Pieces of tin
Masking tape
Small hammer
Center punch
Tin snips
Double-sided adhesive tape

1. Trace the templates for the cards and motifs (pages 96, 97), making sure that you transfer all cutting lines and fold lines, too. The dots on the motif outlines indicate the positions of the punched holes. Cut the basic card shape, then cut out the windows, using a craft knife or scalpel and a metal ruler. Score and fold the card along the fold lines.

2. Choose a motif, then cut a piece of metal about 2.5cm larger all round than the motif. Place the piece of metal on thick card and place the traced motif on top, holding the tracing in place with masking tape. Place the point of the center punch on each dot and tap once or twice with a hammer. The aim is to make a neat dent in the surface of the metal but not to pierce a hole right through. Continue until the motif is complete, then remove the tracing.

94

3. Using the tin-snips, trim the metal so that it is about 1.5cm larger all round than the window cut in the card. Attach the metal, face down behind the window, using double-sided tape to hold it in place.

4. Fold over the left-hand side of the card to cover the back of the metal piece. Hold it in place with double-sided tape.

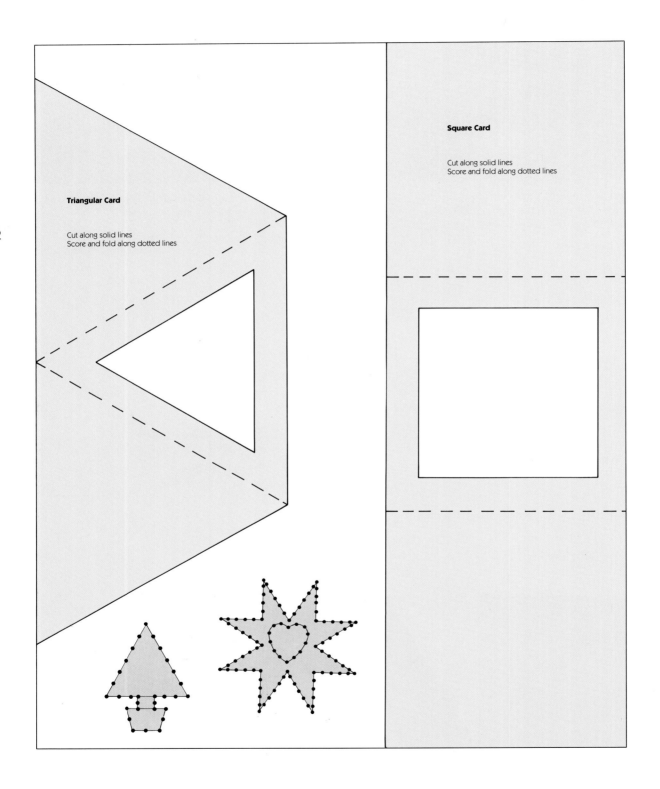

Triangular Card

Cut along solid lines
Score and fold along dotted lines

Square Card

Cut along solid lines
Score and fold along dotted lines

Enlarge all templates by 33% on a photocopier to trace at full size

Rectangular Card

Cut along solid lines
Score and fold along dotted lines

STENCILED INVITATIONS AND PLACE CARDS

Gold on ivory-colored card is a sophisticated combination for these elegant invitation cards and place cards. The patterns are stenciled onto the plain card, but you could also stencil the notifs onto plain paper napkins and even a white tablecloth for a wholly coordinated look. Use a paint that is specially designed for stenciling, because it is quick drying, but remember to wash the brushes, sponges and mixing palette as soon as you have finished, so that the paint does not harden and become almost impossible to remove.

YOU WILL NEED

Tracing paper	Textured paper, such as
Pencil	heavy watercolor paper
Thick card	Gold stencil paint
Clear acetate stencil film	Saucer or palette
Masking tape	Sponge
Scalpel or craft knife	Ruler
Leather punch	Blunt table knife
	Metallic gold pen

98

1. Trace the templates (BELOW LEFT) and place the traced motif on a piece of thick card. Place a piece of acetate film over the tracing and hold the two together with tabs of masking tape. Use a scalpel or craft knife to cut out the design. The star and heart are the easiest to cut out. The holly leaves involve more curved lines, and the most difficult is the little gift. To begin with, cut only the ribbon of the gift.

Heart

Star

Holly

Gift

2. Use a leather punch to cut the tiny dots in the gift stencil. Little holes like this would be impossible to cut in any other way.

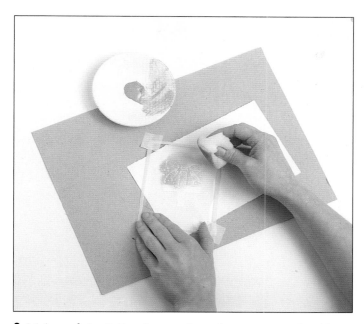

3. Make each invitation from a piece of paper measuring 20 × 11cm. Mark the halfway point lightly with a pencil line. Place the stencil in the center of the left-hand side of the paper. Put a little paint in a saucer or palette. Take a piece of sponge and press the surface onto the paint, taking care that you do not overload the sponge. Press the sponge lightly on the stencil, using a dabbing action. Let the paint dry before you remove the stencil.

4. Beginning at the top of the stenciled pattern, halfway across the front section of the paper, use the scalpel or craft knife to cut carefully around the right-hand side of the design. Stop when you reach the bottom, again about half-way across the front portion.

5. Using a ruler and a blunt table knife, score along the halfway point measured in step 3. Then score halfway across the front section, above and below the stenciled motif but not across the design itself.

6. Fold the paper along the fold lines so that the motif stands out of the folded front part and creates a very simple three-dimensional effect.

7. Make each place card from a square of paper measuring about 12 × 12cm. Mark the halfway point, then stencil the design as before, but position the motif slightly to the left of center. Score across the halfway point, avoiding the stencil. Write a name on the card with a metallic pen, then fold back the top half of the card.

CHRISTMAS STOCKING

Children love finding a stocking of presents on Christmas morning. They are simple to make and you can use any material you have to hand. Decorate them with buttons, beads, and ribbon. Each stocking is approximately 40cm long and 25.5cm wide at the base of the foot.

1. Make the basic stocking in yellow fabric with a contrasting blue checked top and Christmas tree.

2. Use blue checked fabric as the base and add a green top and details in red checked fabric.

3. Make a blue and tartan stocking. Add a tartan pocket and bows made from checked cloth and raffia.

ADVENT CALENDAR

Children will love this Christmas tree Advent calendar, complete with shining star, a host of chirpy robins and a pile of little gifts. Each one hides a box containing candies or a small surprise and has a number to correspond to each of the days up to Christmas.

YOU WILL NEED

Stiff card, green, white, and red
Pencil
Scissors
Double-sided adhesive tape
Double-sided adhesive pads
Dark fiber tip pen
Assorted scraps of paper,
brown, red, black, gold, etc
Scraps of corrugated card (red, green)
Narrow ribbons, assorted colors
Craft knife
Double-sided adhesive Velcro fastening
Adhesive numbers

2. Attach the tree and the pot to the background, using double-sided adhesive pads. This will give a slightly three-dimensional effect.

1. To make the tree and background, trace the template pieces full size, using the grid given on page 105. Each square represents 5cm. First cut out the snow from the white card and use double-sided tape to secure it in place on the large blue background board. Then cut out the pot from red card, and the tree from green.

3. To make the robins, trace the robin template shapes given on page 105. You will need to make 12 robins. Cut the main body in brown, the wings in black, and the chest in red. Remember that the robins need to face each other, so make six that look to the left, and six that look to the right.

4. Assemble the robins, using double-sided adhesive tape.

5. When the robins are complete, draw in the eyes with a dark fiber tip pen.

6. To make the boxes, trace the box tray and sleeve templates on page 105. Cut 24 trays in white card, 13 sleeves in green card and 11 sleeves in white. Score and fold where indicated. Make up the box trays and fix with double-sided tape.

7. Using double-sided tape, attach the green sleeves as shown to the back of the robins and the star, and save the white ones to attach to the gifts (step 8).

103

8. To make the gifts, cut six squares 7 × 7cm and five rectangles 5 × 7cm from stiff white card. Cover the squares and rectangles with scraps of corrugated card etc, then tie each with a ribbon bow. Attach a box to the back of each gift .

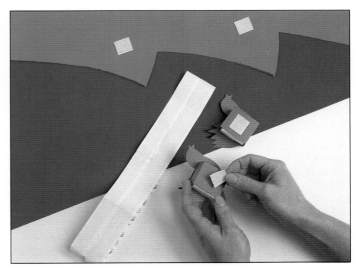

9. Cut 24 pieces of Velcro, each 2cm long. Separate the hook side from the loop side and fix one to the back of each box sleeve and the other to the calendar. Use the photograph as a guide to positioning.

10. Trace the star template given on page 105. Cut out in gold card and attach a box to the back.

11. Stick a number on each of the robins and the gifts but make the star number 24. Secure each piece in place on the calendar, and then count the days to Christmas.

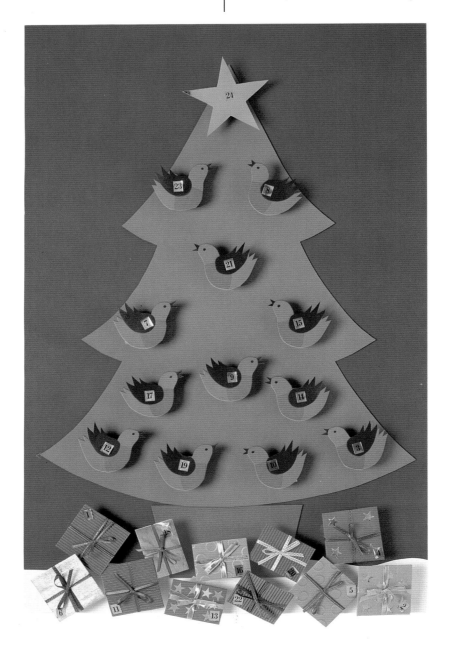

Each square represents 5cm

Robin (Body)
(Brown) x 12

Robin (Wing)
(Black) x 12

Robin (Chest)
(Red) x 12

Cut along solid lines

Score along folded lines

Star x 1

Box Tray

Box Sleeve

Enlarge templates on a photocopier by 33% to trace at full size

NATURAL CHRISTMAS CARDS AND GIFT TAGS

Let nature help when it comes to decorating cards and gift tags. Collect dried fruit slices, spices, leaves, and seeds and arrange them on different kinds of paper. Some of the most successful designs are made simply by lining up spices or seeds in rows or spirals around an interesting shape – a piece of dried fruit or a leaf, for example – so use your imagination to create a multitude of designs. Use a handmade paper with a deckled edge, use a pair of deckle-edged scissors, or tear the edge carefully so that it has the same effect.

YOU WILL NEED

Assorted papers,
    including handmade or
    textured papers
Sharp scissors
Double-sided adhesive
    tape
Quick-drying adhesive
Selection of cloves, tiny
    chiles, sycamore keys,
    dried fruit slices, star
    anise, cinnamon bark,
    dried bay leaves
Paper punch
Fine string or twine

2. Arrange the dried fruit, seeds, and so forth on the front of the card. When you are happy with the arrangement, stick them down with a quick-drying adhesive.

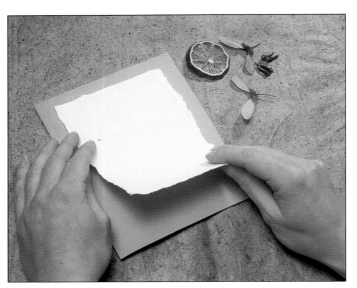

1. Cut a rectangle of paper measuring about 24 × 15cm. Score down the center and fold the paper in half. Take a smaller rectangle of a contrasting paper and fix it to the front with double-sided adhesive tape.

3. Make a matching gift tag in the same way but with a smaller piece of paper – say, a quarter or a third of the size of the main card. Punch a hole in one corner and thread through a length of string or twine so that you can attach the tag to a package.

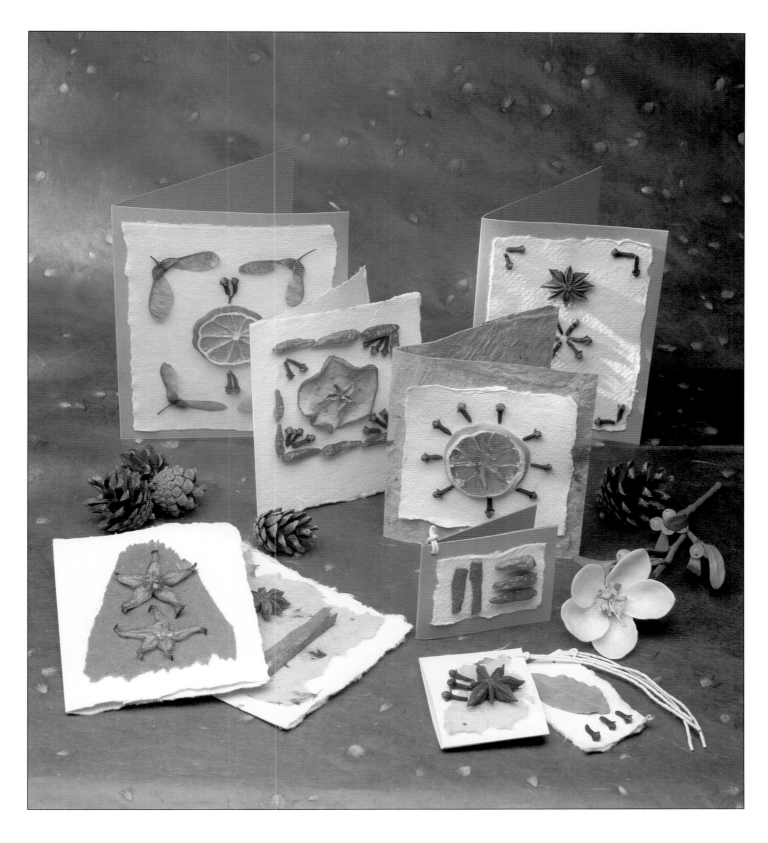

OH, TANNENBAUM

This pop-up tree is a fairly easy card to make, and you can involve your children in coloring the tree and tub when you have cut them out. This tree was decorated with felt-tipped pens, but you could stick on little pieces of paper and self-adhesive stars and spangles. The grid is drawn to a scale of 1:2.

YOU WILL NEED

Backing sheet (thin gray card glued to mounting card), 21.5 × 20cm
Scissors
Adhesive tape

Thin gray card (for tree and tub), about 25 × 15cm
Craft knife or scalpel
Felt-tipped pens
Clear, all-purpose adhesive

KEY

———— cut along this line

———— suggested artwork

———— mountain crease

———— valley crease

[ ] glue here (sometimes on the underside)

Tub

Tree

1. Cut the backing sheet in half, place it face down, butt the cut edges together, and stick them together with tape so that it will lie flat after being folded. Use the template (LEFT) to cut out the tree and tub. Decorate them, then apply glue to the tree tabs.

2. Glue the tree to the backing sheet, making sure that the center of the tree aligns exactly with the center of the card base.

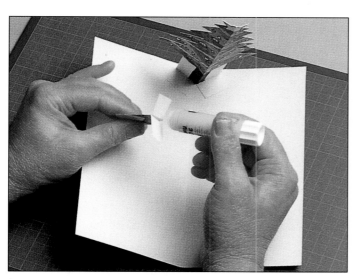

3. Apply glue to the underside of the tub tabs.

4. Glue the tub to the backing sheet, making sure to position it a little way in front of the tree.

5. When the card is shut, the tree and tub will tip forward.

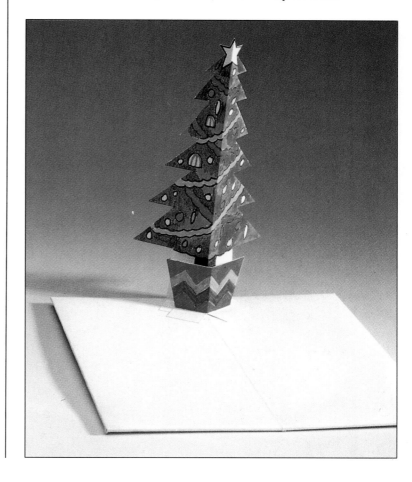

FESTIVE FIR

Although this pop-up design looks simple, the construction must be very precise so that it will work well. In particular, pay attention to the way the base of the tree pieces glue to the inside of the tub, because the measurements and creasing must be absolutely accurate. You will know when you have got it right because the tree will open gracefully.
The grid is drawn to a scale of 1:2½.

YOU WILL NEED

Backing sheet (thin orange card glued to mounting card), 37 × 32cm
Scissors
Adhesive tape
Thick green paper (for tree), about 23 × 20cm
Thick brown paper (for tub), about 20 × 13cm
Craft knife or scalpel
Clear, all-purpose adhesive

KEY

——— cut along this line
——— mountain crease
——— valley crease
▭ glue here (sometimes on the underside)

Tree

Tub

1. Cut the backing sheet in half, place it face down, butt the cut edges together, and stick them with tape so that it will lie flat after being folded. Use the template (LEFT) to cut out the tree pieces and tub. Note the different positions of the slits on the two tree halves.

2. Slide the tree pieces together to interlock the slits.

3. Apply glue to the end tab on the tub, then form it into a square tube.

4. Apply glue to the four tabs at the base of the tree.

6. Apply glue to the underside of the tub tabs, then stick the tabs to the backing sheet.

5. Glue the tree inside the tub so that the crease on each tree tab lies exactly down the center of each tub face.

7. Although it is very three-dimensional, the tub and tree will easily collapse flat when the card is closed.

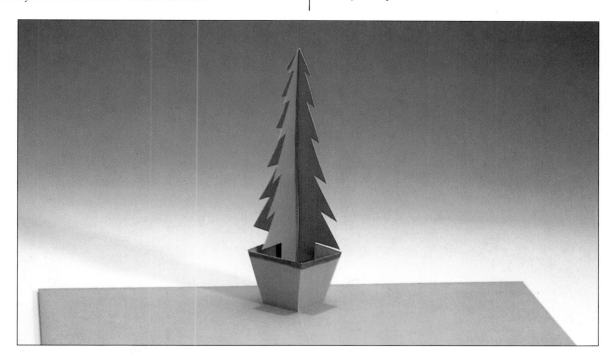

WHERE'S RUDOLPH?

The crease pattern used here to make Santa Claus open out will be familiar to anyone who has ever made an origami water-bomb. Indeed, many origami bases and techniques can be adapted for use in pop-up designs. A close study of the similarities between the two papercrafts can be the source of many inspirational ideas. For best results, place the three creases that run across the figure of Santa Claus very precisely. It would be worth making a rough, undecorated figure to judge the placement of the creases before folding the actual figure.
The grid is drawn to a scale of 1:2.

YOU WILL NEED

Backing sheet (thin blue card glued to mounting card), 39.5 × 19cm
Scissors
Adhesive tape
Craft knife or scalpel

Medium weight white paper (for Santa Claus), about 28 × 15cm
Felt-tipped pens or marker pens
Clear, all-purpose adhesive

112

KEY

▬▬▬	cut along this line
┈┈┈	suggested artwork
▬▬▬	mountain crease

▬ ▬ ▬	valley crease
▭	glue here (sometimes on the underside)

1. Cut the backing sheet in half, place it face down, butt the cut edges together, and stick them together with tape so that it will lie flat after being folded. Use the template (LEFT) to cut out the figure of Santa Claus. Crease the figure down the center. Open it out.

2. With the decorated side upward, crease one of the diagonals. Open out.

3. Repeat, folding the other diagonal. Both diagonals must cross the center crease at the same point.

4. Santa will collapse along the creases.

6. Glue the hands to the backing sheet.

5. Apply glue to the underside of both hands.

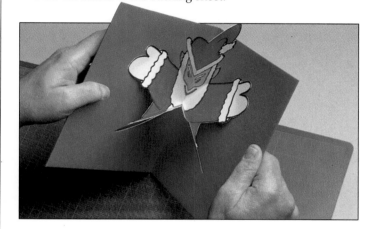

7. Note that the card will not open absolutely flat.

TWO-PIECE BOXES

A two-piece box can be a simple tray or it can be a complicated star-shaped box – ideal for a little Christmas gift. Use a fairly stiff card, and either cover it when it is finished or decorate the card before cutting it out.

BASIC BOX

1. The most basic box that you can possibly make is to cut out a cruciform shape to the required size and to stick the sides together with adhesive tape.

2. Make the lid in the same way, but make the sides very short and add about 0.2cm (depending on the thickness of the card you are using) to the dimensions in all directions so that the lid will slip over the sides of the box.

3. A slightly more sophisticated box is made with glued tabs. Make sure that you make the allowance for the lid slightly more than for the simple tray box to accommodate the extra thickness of the flaps

WRAP-ROUND BOX

1. Make a wrap-round box by marking a strip of card that is equal in length to twice the length and twice the width of the gift, plus a glue flap. The strip can have joins if necessary. Cut out the card, score the folds, and glue to form a box.

2. The wrap-round lid is made from a piece of card measuring the length of the gift by twice the width and twice the height plus an overlap. Cut out and score the folds.

3. Glue the center section of the lid to the glue flap at the base of the box. Fold the side and top pieces around the box, enclosing the gift. Either tie it to close or seal with a sticker.

STAR-SHAPED BOX

1. Mark out a strip of card, but with the sides of equal length, to form a square. Make the lid in the same way, but slightly larger.

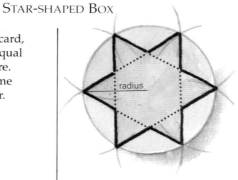

2. To construct the star, measure the length of one side of the box with the compasses to find the radius of the circle. Draw the circle, and, keeping the same radius setting, place the point of the compasses on the circumference of the circle, and mark the point it crosses on the curve. Move the compass to this point, and repeat the process until you have six points around the circumference. Join alternate points with a pencil and ruler.

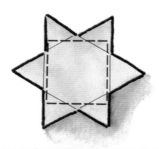

3. Cut out two star shapes and glue one to the flaps of the base, and the other to the flaps of the top of the lid.

115

The possibilities for decorating homemade boxes are endless. Decorative adhesive tape, stickers, and attractive ties all contribute to a professional looking gift. The basket-type box was made by weaving strips of metallic-finish card together, with a simple strip attached to act as a handle.

SIMPLE GIFT WRAPS

This is a simple technique for decorating paper, and is suitable for children to try. You can transform sheets of plain, matt construction paper into richly patterned, unusual wrapping paper with very few materials. Gold and red or green always look festive, but you could use silver or red or purple. Remember to finish off the present with matching ribbon.

YOU WILL NEED

Large sheets of plain poster paper
Gold poster or acrylic craft paint

Saucer or palette
Cloth or tissue paper
Low-tack masking tape
Metallic gold spray paint

116

1. Lay the sheet of paper on a flat surface. Pour a small amount of gold paint into a saucer or mixing palette. Take a piece of cloth or tissue paper, about 20 ×20cm, and crumple it in your hand. Press the crumpled surface onto the paint in the saucer, taking particular care not to overload the paper or cloth with paint.

3. For a striped effect, lay a sheet of plain paper on a flat surface. Place masking tape in diagonal stripes, about 2.5cm apart, across it.

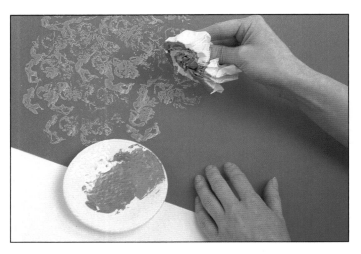

2. Press the paint-coated surface onto the paper to create a mottled pattern. Work all over the surface of the paper with a light, dabbing action. Make sure that you do not smudge the paint as you work.

4. Use the mottling technique described in steps 1 and 2 to apply random splodges of gold paint over the surface of the paper. Leave to dry before removing the masking tape.

5. If you prefer checks to stripes, fold a sheet of poster paper concertina style, with each fold about 2cm wide. To protect your work surface cover with newspaper. Stretch out the paper a little on your work top and use a metal gold spray paint to coat the paper with a fine mist of paint. Spray from one angle only, so that one side of each fold catches the paint creating a striped effect when the paper is opened out.

6. When the paint is completely dry, repeat the process, but this time making the folds at right angles to the first folds.

7. Add a special finishing touch to the present with matching gift tags and pretty folded fans.

CHRISTMAS CRACKERS

Crackers are a traditional part of Christmas, but they do not simply have to contain a little plastic trinket and a paper hat. You could put any small gift – no matter how expensive – in the middle of these festive crackers. The first project is simply an alternative way of wrapping a small gift. The second will make your festivities go with a bang!

TARTAN CRACKERS

YOU WILL NEED

Thin card, 23 × 18cm
Tartan paper, 34 × 18cm
About 60cm paper lace
Clear, all-purpose adhesive
Double-sided adhesive tape

Fine string or strong thread
Fine-gauge wire
Paper ribbon bows (optional)
Sprigs of heather (optional)

1. Cut the thin card into three pieces, one measuring 18 × 9cm and two measuring 18 × 7cm. Form the two smaller pieces into tubes. Stick paper lace along the short edges of the tartan paper.

2. Roll the larger piece of card into a tube and place it in the center of the paper. Insert your gift and fasten the paper around the tube, using double-sided tape. Tie the paper with string or thread at the ends of the central tube, then open out the ends and insert the small tubes into the ends.

3. Thread some fine wire through lengths of paper lace and gather it up. Tie it around the joints in the cracker, twisting the wire together firmly to hold it in place. Decorate the cracker with paper ribbon bows and sprigs of heather if wished.

TRADITIONAL CRACKERS

YOU WILL NEED

Tracing paper
White card
Metallic finish crepe paper
in colors of your choice
Scissors
Pinking shears
Pencil

Double-sided adhesive tape
3 inner tubes from rolls of
toilet tissue
Cracker snap
Narrow ribbon to match
paper

1. Copy the template (page 121) and transfer the outline to a piece of white card. Cut a rectangle, 34 × 18cm, from one of the colors of crepe paper, and two pieces, each 18 × 16cm, from a contrasting color. Always cut crepe paper so that the grain runs along the length of the cracker. Use pinking shears to trim both ends of the large rectangle. Fold the smaller pieces in half, matching the 18cm sides, and place a template to the fold in the paper. Use a pencil to draw all around the template.

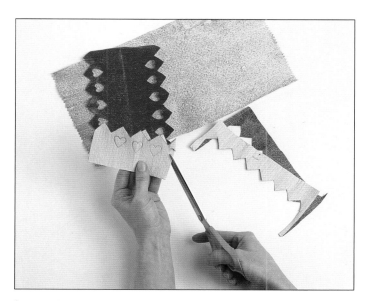

2. Use sharp pointed scissors to cut out the shapes from the smaller rectangles.

3. Position the contrasting pieces about 2.5cm in from the ends of the larger piece and stick in place with strips of double-sided adhesive tape.

4. Trim the cardboard tubes so that one is 11cm long and the other two are 6cm long. Turn over the crepe paper and place the long tube in the center, with the other two tubes about 1.5cm from the pinked edges. Slip the cracker snap inside the tubes, and place a gift or some wrapped candy in the center tube.

5. Wrap the crepe paper around the tubes, and use double-sided adhesive tape to stick the crepe paper firmly in place.

6. Hold the center of the cracker in one hand and one end in your other hand. Gently twist the cracker clockwise, then anticlockwise. This creases the paper between the tubes and makes it easier to tie in the next step.

7. Take a short length of matching ribbon and tie the cracker tightly around the creased part. Trim off the ends of the ribbon. Fasten the other end in the same way.

Christmas Crackers

Place to fold of paper

Christmas Crackers

Place to fold of paper

Christmas Crackers

Place to fold of paper

BLUE AND GOLD

When you want to give a present to someone extra special, an elegant and beautiful decoration on a simply wrapped gift can make it unforgettable. The leaves used here are silk, fastened to wire stems. The little baubles and tree decorations have also been wired, while the contrast is provided by little pieces of Finland moss.

YOU WILL NEED

Gold ribbon to tie around
    parcel and make bow
Scissors
Wire cutters
Finland moss

Selection of silk leaves,
    baubles, decorations,
    all wired
Low-melt glue and glue
    pan

---

1. Wrap the parcel and bind it lengthways with gold ribbon, sealing the ends with a spot of glue or double-sided tape.

2. Make a bow, adding four loops to each side, and stick it on the band of gold ribbon, positioning it where the ribbon ends finish to hide the join.

3. Use wire cutters to trim the ends of the wires and glue the leaves into the center of the bow. Add the decorative parcel and gold balls and berries. To finish, dip small pieces of Finland moss in the glue and tuck them well into the design.

FANCY DRESS

Make a plain box a gift in its own right by decorating it to look like something else. Use your imagination to create a costume appropriate to the recipient of the gift, and use any of the paper techniques – pleating, folding, curling, and cutting – to create a truly original wrapping. For a New Year gift, wrapping the gifts in evening dress seemed appropriate.

YOU WILL NEED

Colored and plain white,   Glue stick
    black, and gray papers   Felt-tipped pens
Double-sided tape   Buttons

124

1. Wrap the box in plain white paper. Cut strips of gray paper about 1.5cm wide.

2. Wrap black paper around the parcel so that it meets at the center front, and turn back the corners for the lapels. Stick the gray stripes along the bottom edge to form the shape of the pocket.

3. Cut out two bow tie shapes and stick them together with a piece of tape. Decorate the tie and stick it in place. Add a flower, buttons, and a label.

BOTTLE WITH A DIFFERENCE

What could be better to welcome in the New Year than a bottle of champagne, and if you are visiting friends or staying with relatives, this decorated bottle would be the perfect gift. The flowers and leaves are silk, and they are attached to the side of the bottle with a small piece of dry floral foam (Oasis), known as a mini-deco. These little semicircular pads are especially designed to allow you to create miniature displays on the sides of bottles or even cakes.

YOU WILL NEED

Oasis mini-deco
Selection of assorted silk
    foliage, including ferns
Bere grass
Silk Christmas roses
Low-melt glue and glue
    pan
Gold bow with wire
Finland moss

126

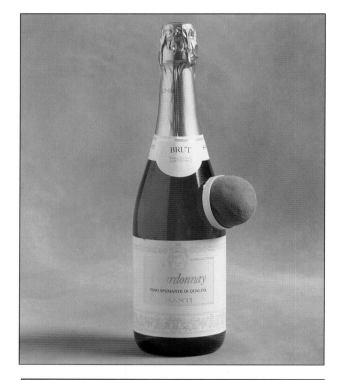

1. Make sure that the surface of the bottle is absolutely clean. Peel off the circle of backing paper from the mini-deco and press it firmly on the surface of the bottle.

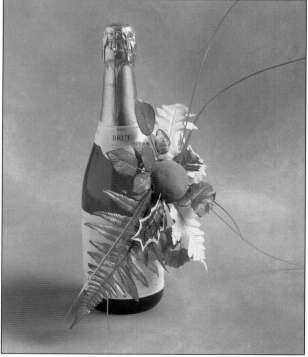

2. Insert small pieces of foliage around the edge of the mini-deco, adding some strands of bere grass around the edge.

3. Dip the ends of the Christmas roses in glue before positioning them. Dip the wire of the bow in the glue and add it in the center of the arrangement. Put a spot of glue on the ends of the bere grass and bend them over toward the center to form loops. Mask any foam that is still visible with clumps of moss.

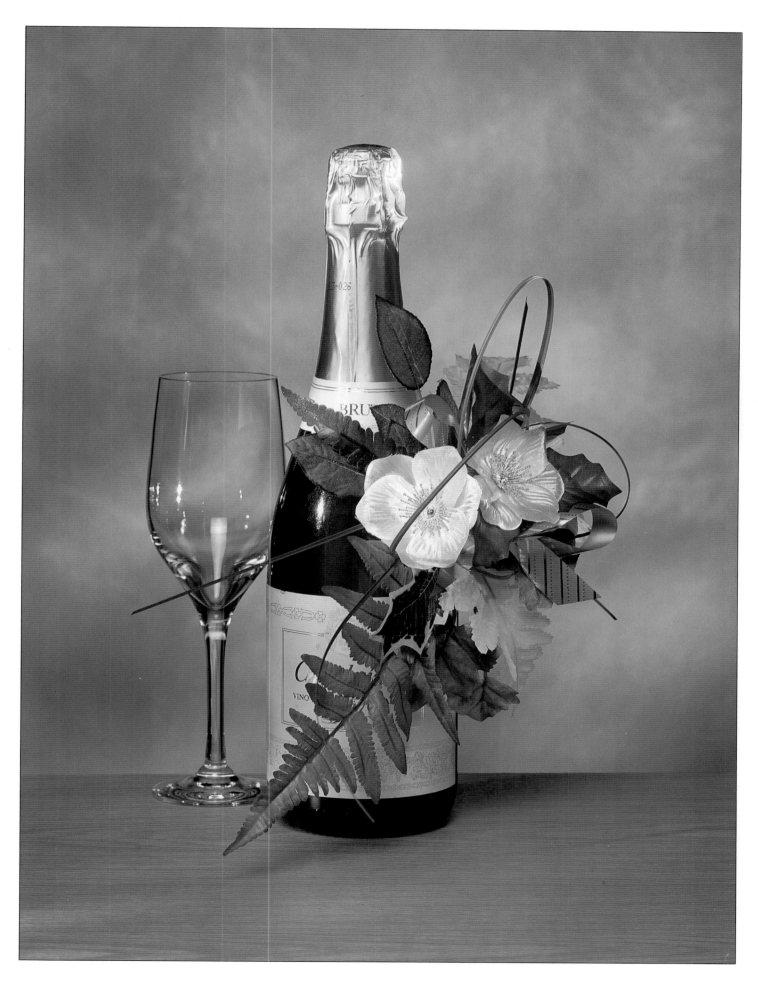

EASTER, HALLOWEEN, AND HARVEST

Why use only conventional papers and ribbons when you are wrapping gifts? In this section we concentrate on ideas for using natural materials, not only as a source of inspiration for unusual gift-wrapping ideas but also as the base materials for the wrapping itself.

Seeds, pods, spices, and many fruits dry easily and quickly. They make fragrant and beautiful additions to your gifts (as well as excellent Christmas tree decorations). Fall is the ideal time to begin to prepare fruit and spices so that you have a wealth of material that can be used later in the year and that will keep until spring. A single layer of citrus slices and spices kept in a warm, dry place will be ready to use in three or four weeks. Fresh and dried herbs and spices can be bought in supermarkets and specialist food stores, and you can coordinate this natural look by using green and brown boxes, raffia, and string.

Leaves are a wonderful form of natural decoration. They come in all shapes, sizes, and colors, and, best of all, they are completely free. Collect leaves all year round. Place them between layers of smooth tissue paper, surround them with newspaper, then weight them down with books for about two weeks.

COVERED BOXES

Boxes can be reused. Chocolate and soap boxes are often especially suitable for use with other gifts, and it is often necessary only to cover the top of the lid, but the same method can be used to cover the bottom too.

YOU WILL NEED
Ruler Paper Scissors Glue stick

1. Measure the width and length of the box lid and the height of the box sides. The piece of paper will have to be large enough for the lid measurement plus four times the sides. Draw the rectangle in the center of a piece of lightweight paper. Add sides all round, and then add another set of sides to turn under. Draw "ears" as shown.

2. Cut out, score, and fold the whole shape. Position the box on the drawn rectangle and turn the "ears" inwards.

3. Stick the "ears" and the turn-in allowance down.

4. Stick down the opposite sides firmly.

LEFT: *Interesting patterns can be made from corrugated card. Always cut the card with a sharp knife from the wrong (flat) side, but do not press too hard so that you do not flatten the ribs. Use a fairly strong adhesive. Cover the top first and then, with the covered top downwards, wrap a strip of corrugated paper around the sides.*

WOVEN PAPER

Weaving is another simple technique that can be used to great effect, whether you use it for small tags and cards, or for larger things, such as the bag shown here. Use any type of paper you have to hand – newsprint, crepe paper, tissue paper, or even handmade paper. You can achieve a range of effects by weaving only parts of the paper or by using a mixture of colors and widths.

YOU WILL NEED

Colored paper
Scissors

Craft knife or scalpel
Ruler

---

1. Cut some colored paper into the shape of a tag. Cut several narrow strips in contrasting colors for the weaving.

2. Cut a series of regularly spaced slits in the tag. Weave the first strip over and under the slits, then weave the second strip under and over. Leave the ends different lengths, or trim them off neatly.

BELOW: To make the woven newspaper bag, fold some newspaper into strips about 1.5cm and pin a row of strips about 1.5cm apart to a thick piece of cardboard, Weave other strips in and out, alternately, to form a flat sheet. Fold the sheet in half and glue the sides together to make a bag. Tape paper ribbon handles to the top before filling with raffia, eggs, and your gift. Fill natural and colored woven baskets with shredded tissue, straw, and a mixture of hand-painted and chocolate eggs.

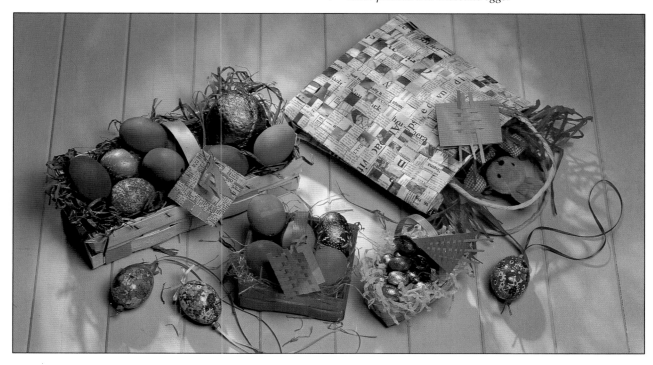

FALL LEAVES

You can produce a wide variety of designs using either natural prints or stencils, and the two techniques are combined in this card, which has an attractive leaf motif.

YOU WILL NEED

Leaves (any fairly flat
  leaves will do)
Paintbrush
Gouache paint: red
Palette or saucer
Sheets of sugar paper,
  29 × 21cm: red, cream

Double-sided adhesive
  tape
Gold spray
Clear, all-purpose adhesive
Cream card, about 30 ×
  20cm
Fine gold pen

132

1. Choose a suitable leaf, then trim off the stalk if necessary. Paint the underside of the leaf, where the veins are prominent, with red gouache paint.

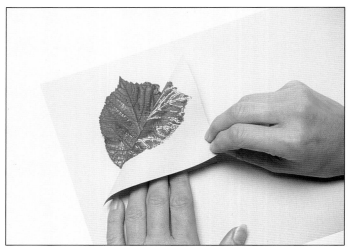

3. Carefully peel back the top sheet of paper to reveal the print. This process can be repeated several times if you wish.

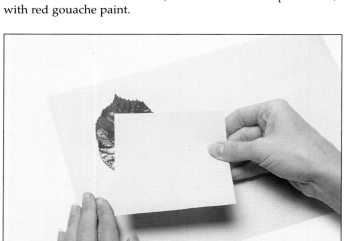

2. Place the leaf on a sheet of paper with the painted side facing upward. Put another piece over the leaf, and press down. Rub over the area.

4. Select several leaves of the same kind and place them in a random pattern on a sheet of colored paper. Hold them in place with small pieces of adhesive tape. Spray over the leaves, ideally using an old cardboard box to protect your working area. Leave to dry for 5 minutes.

5. When the paint is dry, carefully remove the leaves from the paper.

6. Cut the background to size and glue it to a larger, folded piece of contrasting colored card.

7. Tear the leaf print to size, using a ruler to help tear a neat edge, and decorate the torn edges with a gold pen.

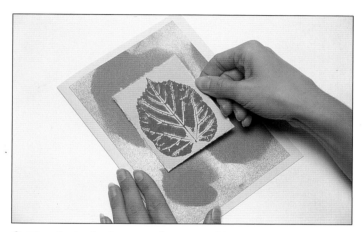

8. Glue the leaf print on to the sprayed background to complete the card.

STENCILED LEAVES

The key to stenciling is to use a dry brush, which will not only give the best results but will help the stencil to last longer. Presents wrapped in paper decorated with these natural shapes will look good tied with string, raffia, or paper ribbon, and you can use scraps of decorated paper to add interest to a plainly wrapped parcel.

YOU WILL NEED

Leaves
Medium weight paper
Sharp pointed scissors or
   scalpel

Stencil or gouache paint in
   shades of green
Saucer or palette
Stencil brush

134

1. Choose an interestingly shaped leaf and draw around it on a sheet of medium weight paper. If you intend to reuse the stencil for several sheets, use a more robust material such as acetate.

2. Carefully cut out the leaf. If you want a perfectly symmetrical shape, fold the paper in half and cut both sides together. In nature, though, leaves are more often slightly asymmetric.

3. Mix the paint to a thick consistency and keep the brush as dry as possible. Lay the stencil over the paper and evenly dab on the paint.

Real leaves can be used as templates for cutting shapes out of brown paper to use for tags. Paint or spatter the leaf shapes with gouache or poster paint, or leave them brown. Punch a hole in the tag, and thread through string or raffia and tie to the wrapped present.

SPATTERING

Spattering is a simple decorative technique. You need a selection of gouache or poster paints, paper, and an old toothbrush or stencil brush. The gifts have been wrapped in brown paper that was spattered with paint, they were then tied with raffia and string, and decorated with real leaves and paper cut-outs, spattered with paint. Dried twigs and berries were added for the final embellishment.

YOU WILL NEED	
Medium weight paper or acetate	Gouache or poster paint
Leaves	Old toothbrush or stencil brush

1. Use a real leaf to make a template from medium weight paper or acetate. Mix the paints to a medium consistency and to produce various shades of green, brown, and gold.

2. Dip the brush into the first color and run your finger across the bristles to produce a fine spray effect. Repeat with other colors. Punch a hole and add a raffia or string tie.

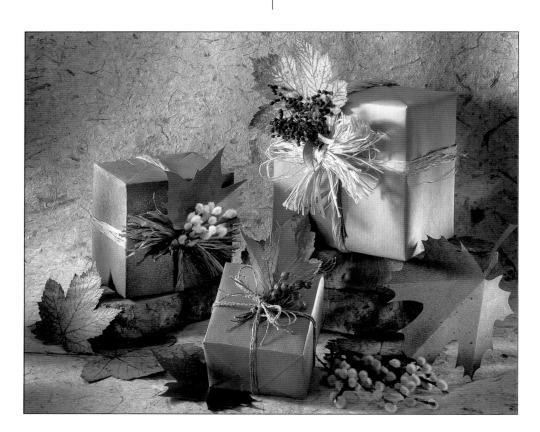

WICKED WITCH

This pop-up design has height and opens with an appropriately large, sweeping movement that will always be remembered. The construction is simple, but the stick supporting the witch must be strong, and the V-angle that it forms at the base must be carefully adjusted so that the witch collapses into the front corner of the card. The grid is drawn to a scale of 1:2½.

YOU WILL NEED

Backing sheet (thin blue card glued to mounting card), 39 × 22cm
Adhesive tape
Thin blue card (for support), about 20 × 6cm
Scissors

Thick black paper (for witch), about 15 × 15cm
Medium weight white paper (for clouds), about 15 × 15cm
Craft knife or scalpel
Clear, all-purpose adhesive

1. Cut the backing sheet in half, place it face down, butt the cut edges together, and stick them together with tape so that it will lie flat after being folded. Use the template (LEFT) to cut out the pieces. Apply glue to the outer, long panels of the support, then fold them inward so that they align with the center crease, halving the width, and doubling the thickness of the support.

Witch

Support

2. Apply glue to the end tabs.

KEY

——— cut along this line

- - - mountain crease

——— valley crease

⬚ glue here (sometimes on the underside)

3. Glue the tabs to the backing sheet.

137

4. Glue the witch to the top of the stick.

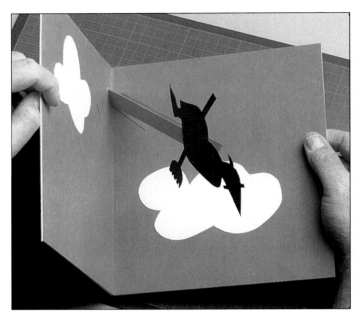

5. If the angle of the fold in step 3 is carefully judged, the witch will collapse into the front corner of the backing sheet when the card is shut.

138

FLAT GIFT-HOLDER

This type of box is most suitable for gifts such as scarves and ties, which need to be folded neatly and kept flat. The boxes can be decorated in a variety of ways.

Measure the gift, then make the holder the length of the gift. If the gift is solid, allow a little extra. At its deepest point, the curves at the top and bottom of the holder should measure approximately twice the height of the gift.

With these measurements, it is now possible to draw the plan of the gift holder (see diagram). The curve can either be drawn with compasses, placed on the center line, or by using a dinner plate of a suitable size. Join two sides with one curve, and trace this off on a piece of scrap card. Use this as a template to draw the other curves. Cut out and score the card. Stick the glue flap to the side. Place the gift in the holder and close by turning in the curves.

BELOW: The blue gift holder is decorated with a cut-out butterfly shape. The green one was made with lightweight card that was decorated with a stenciled design.

PYRAMID BOX

This little box can either be used to contain a gift or as decoration on it – the size can be varied as you wish depending on the gift that you have to wrap.

YOU WILL NEED

Sheet of card   Ruler
Pencil   Glue stick
Pair of compasses   Craft knife / scalpel

1. Draw a line the length of the base of one side. Draw a semicircle on the line. Place the compass point, with the same radius, at one end of the semicircle and mark the center and the point it crosses on the curve.

2. Repeat from the other end of the line.

3. With the same radius setting, draw another semicircle so that it joins the first.

4. Put the compass point on the join and mark the point it crosses on this curve. Join all the marks, and you will have four equilateral triangles.

5. Add a glue flap to the base of the first triangle, two tucking flaps with slits, and two tabs to correspond to the slits.

6. Cut out the basic shape and score all the other lines.

7. Stick the glue flap and place the gift inside and close the box tightly with the tabs. Although it is tricky to tuck in the tabs, they do give a very secure closure.

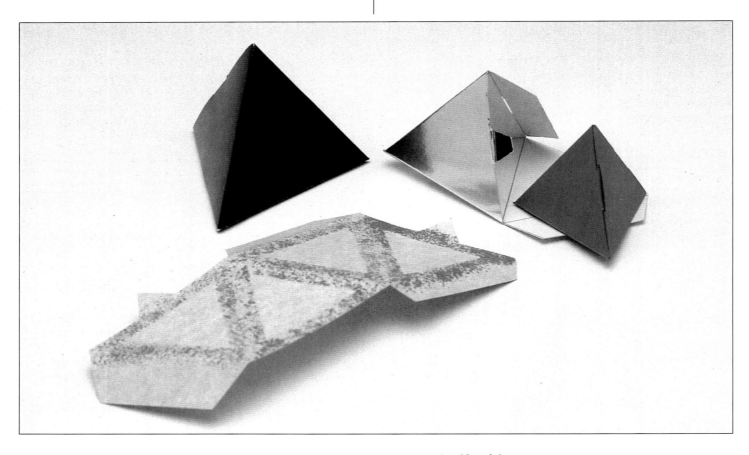

You can make a pyramid box that is any size. Use plain or foiled card, or decorate plain card with stencils or by spattering.

SEE-THROUGH SOLUTION

Here is a pretty and practical solution to the perennial problem of wrapping a spherical gift.

YOU WILL NEED

Tissue paper
Fine string or strong
 thread
Cellophane or acetate
Craft ribbon

1. Place the gift on a large square of brightly colored tissue paper. Bring the edges to the top.

2. Tie tightly with a piece of strong thread, and spread out the bunched-up paper at the top.

3. Cover the wrapped gift in the same way, but this time with crisp acetate or cellophane. Tie it with another piece of thread.

4. Finish off with a bright length of ribbon in a contrasting color and tie a neat bow. Alternatively, add a tassel or attach some beads to some colored cord.

141

MESSAGE IN THE BOTTLE

A corrugated cardboard tube is an excellent way of wrapping a bottle and it can look surprisingly decorative. Use plain or colored, stiff, corrugated cardboard or any thick, bendable card.

YOU WILL NEED

Corrugated cardboard
Craft knife or scissors
Strong adhesive or
 double-sided adhesive
 tape
Plain card
Narrow ribbon to decorate

1. Measure the circumference and height of the bottle and cut the cardboard so that it is a little taller than the bottle and will wrap around it, overlapping by about 0.5cm.

2. Glue or use double-sided tape to stick the sides of the cardboard together to make a tube.

3. Cut out a round piece of thick, non-corrugated card for the base and glue it to the bottom of the tube. You may find it easier to make four small tabs of thin card, which you can use to attach the base to the tube.

4. Cut a piece of corrugated cardboard for the lid. It should fit tightly over the main tube but be loose enough to slide on easily. Glue or tape the edges together to form a tube.

5. Cut a second circle from thick, non-corrugated card for the top of the lid and glue or tape it in place.

6. Put the bottle inside the tube, slide on the lid, and tie securely with narrow ribbon.

Good Luck and
— Congratulations —

In this section are some ideas for those occasions when you want to give someone a little gift to wish them well or send a card to show that you are thinking of them. Moving house, for example, is one of the most stressful things that a family can do, so how better to welcome your friends or relatives to their new home than by sending a handmade card or a thoughtfully packaged little gift?

Cover empty chocolate or tea-bag boxes with shop-bought gift-wrap, or cover your presents with colorful tissue paper. Decorate the gifts with shredded paper for a colorful and unusual alternative to a ribbon bow. Experiment with cellophane, which can be used to cover plain, bright colors, giving an extra sparkle and sheen to a brilliant primary shade, and look out for patterned cellophane, which is available with colorful spots and squiggles over the surface.

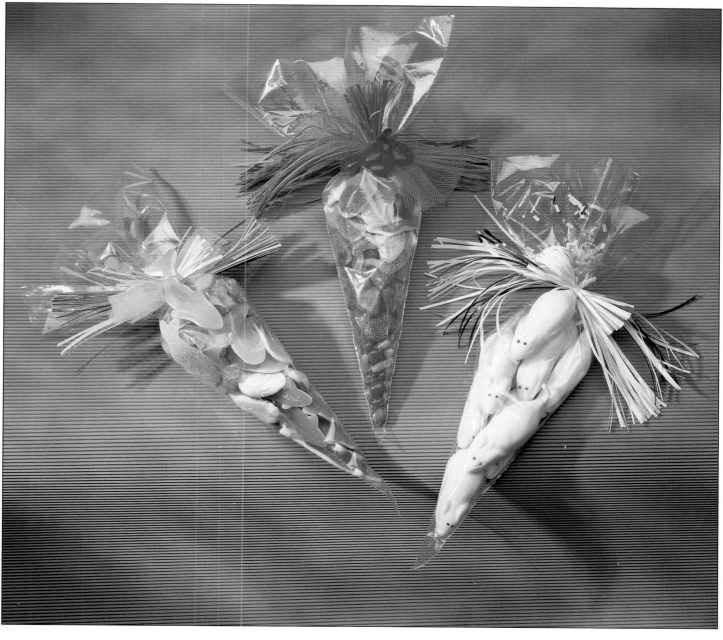

WAX RESIST CARD

This is an ideal technique for children, and it works especially well with fairly simple motifs such as flowers, hearts, and animals. It has been used here to make a card to welcome someone to a new home.

YOU WILL NEED

White wax crayon or
    candle
Watercolor paper
Paintbrushes
Gouache paints: orange,
    red, yellow

Clear, all-purpose
    adhesive or double-sided
    adhesive tape
Colored card, 30 × 13cm
Scissors

144

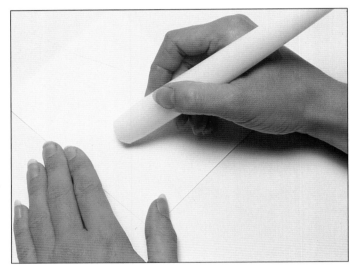

1. Draw the design on watercolor paper using a candle or white wax crayon. If you tilt the paper slightly in the light you can see the lines you have drawn.

2. Take a brush loaded with paint and apply it to the paper. For best results, limit the number of colors you use, although it is possible to mix them on the paper to get different shades.

3. Blend the paints together on the paper with a clean brush and water. Leave to dry for 10–20 minutes.

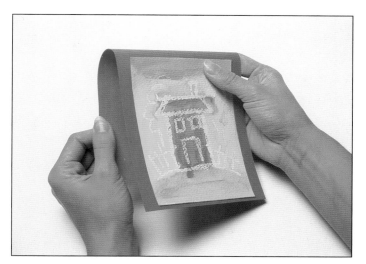

4. When the paint is completely dry, use adhesive or double-sided tape to stick the design to the large piece of contrasting colored card.

5. Fold the card in half so that the image appears on the front of the card.

145

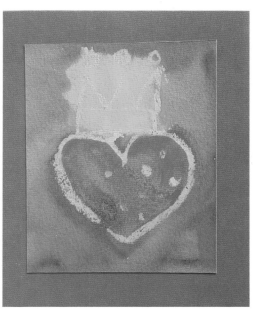

START PACKING

A design such as this can be varied in as many ways as you want — you can design it to suit a particular family, perhaps by including a piano, or some favorite toys or pieces of furniture, or a pet dog. If you use this pattern, add some humorous labels to the boxes. Often, the more a card is personalized — and the less like a shop-bought card it looks — the more it is appreciated. The grid is drawn to a scale of 1:2½.

YOU WILL NEED

Backing sheet (thin
  mottled brown card),
  28 × 21cm
Adhesive tape

Thin mottled brown card
  (for supports and
  packing cases), about
  46 × 20cm

Scissors
Fine black felt-tipped pen
Craft knife or scalpel
Clear, all-purpose adhesive

146

1. Cut the backing sheet in half, place it face down, butt the cut edges together, and stick them together with tape so that it will lie flat after being folded. Use the template (ABOVE) to cut out the pieces. Apply glue to both ends of tab A.

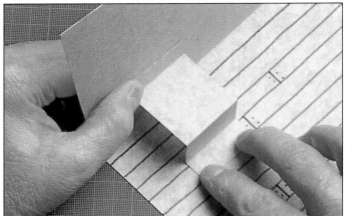

2. Position it at the left of the backing sheet.

3. Apply the other tabs in the same way, checking the alignment of each.

5. Repeat step 4 for cases B, C, and D.

4. Glue packing case A onto tab A.

6. Redraw the black lines of the tabs.

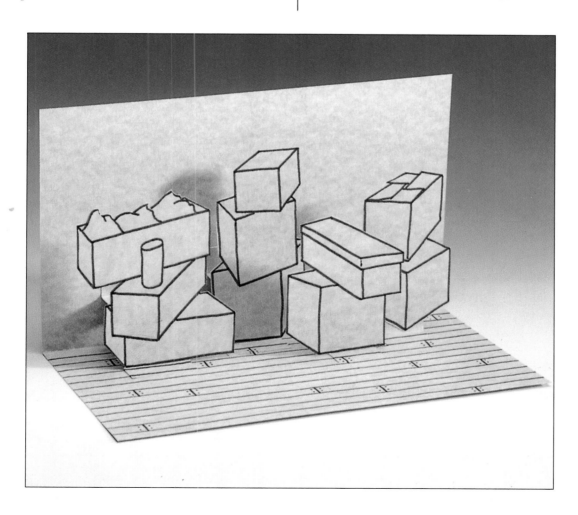

FUN REMOVALS

The van in this design is a modified box, but the pop-up element lies parallel to the backing sheet, not at an angle. Using this adaptable technique, a whole fleet of vehicles could be constructed, as well as boats, ships, and airplanes. The sides of the van can be enlivened by adding an apposite name. The grid is drawn to a scale of 1:2.

KEY

▬▬▬	cut along this line
▭▭▭	suggested artwork
▬ ▬ ▬	mountain crease
▬▬ ▬▬	valley crease
▭	glue here (sometimes on the underside)
‒‒‒ ‒‒‒	these measurements are the same

YOU WILL NEED

Backing sheet (thin pink card glued to mounting card), 22 × 17cm
Adhesive tape
Scissors

Thin green card (for van), about 36 × 15cm
Craft knife or scalpel
Clear, all-purpose adhesive

148

1. Cut the backing sheet in half, place it face down, butt the cut edges together, and stick them together with tape so that it will lie flat after being folded. Use the template (ABOVE) to cut out the van. Make all the creases.

2. Apply glue to the end tab and glue it into the vehicle.

3. Glue in the two top tabs.

5. Push the tabs through the slits and tape them flat to the reverse of the backing sheet.

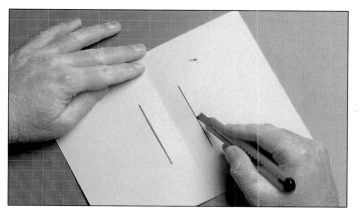

4. Make the slits in the backing sheet. The distance between them is the width of the van.

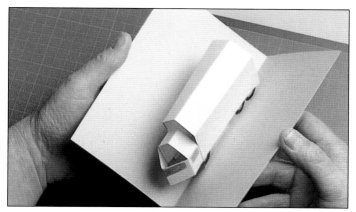

6. Note how the vehicle opens and flattens when the card is folded flat.

NEW HOME, SWEET HOME

This is a complicated card to make, but it looks so good that you will want to try it if you have successfully attempted any of the other pop-up designs in this book. The house is made in the form of a box, as is the fence. The telegraph pole is attached to the fence, and the chimney is not attached to the roof, but to the backing sheet, which increases the three-dimensional effect. The grid is drawn to a scale of 1:2½.

YOU WILL NEED

Backing sheet (white
mounting card),
30 × 22cm
Adhesive tape
Thin green, brown, dark
green, gray, and white
card (for all other

pieces), about 30 × 25cm
in total
Scissors
Craft knife or scalpel
Clear, all-purpose adhesive
Masking tape

KEY

———— cut along this line

‑ ‑ ‑ ‑ suggested artwork

———— mountain crease

———— valley crease

▭ glue here (sometimes
on the underside)

150

1. Cut the backing sheet in half, place it face down, butt the cut edges together, and stick them together with tape so that it will lie flat after being folded. Use the template (ABOVE) to cut out the pieces. Apply glue to both ends of the tree strap.

2. Glue the strap across the central crease on the backing sheet. The strap folds up when the card is closed.

3. Glue the tree to one end of the strap.

4. Glue and fold the chimney so that it is double thickness, and glue its tabs to the backing sheet, each side of the central crease.

5. Glue the tab at the end of the house to the other end to make it three-dimensional.

6. Add masking tape to the long top edges of the house, then lower on the roof. Fix it in place so that it rests in the correct position. This may take several attempts, and you will need to open out the house to check that you have got it right.

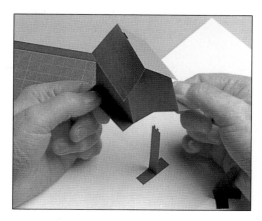

7. Apply glue to the underside of the house tabs.

8. Glue them to the backing sheet, taking care to lower the house over the chimney and to pull the house fully open.

9. Similarly, fold and glue the fence to the backing sheet. Stretch it so that it is square.

11. When the card is closed, all the separate pieces collapse.

10. Glue the telegraph pole to the fence and backing sheet. Assemble the telegraph pole and cross-pieces and glue to the front of the tab.

HEXAGONAL BOX

This box looks most impressive, but it is not as complicated to make as it appears. Once the size of the hexagon has been decided upon, it is quite easy to construct. If the box is being used for a circular gift, make sure that this fits within the hexagon.

YOU WILL NEED

Sheet of card
Pair of compasses
Pencil
Ruler
Scissors
Glue stick

BELOW: This hexagonal box was made using embossed foil card. Filled with foil-wrapped chocolates, it makes an impressive gift.

153

1. Draw a circle larger than the gift. Draw a horizontal line through the center of the circle.

2. Using the same radius setting, place the compass point on one of the intersections and mark the point it crosses on the curve.

3. Move the compass to this point, and repeat until you have six points around the circumference.

4. Join these points and check again that the gift will fit in the base of the box. Then draw a plan, using the diagram as a guide.

5. The sides of the box are equal to the height of the gift and one side of the hexagon in length. The three flaps, top and bottom, are half the height of the hexagon.

6. Cut out and score the box. Fold the pieces. Check the angles before gluing the flaps in case any adjustments are necessary.

7. Stick the glue flap and assemble the box. If necessary, stick down the tucking flaps on the base so that the box does not fall apart if the gift is heavy.

BROWN PAPER CARDS

This technique was discovered while experimenting with inks and brown parcel paper. You can use it to produce one-off pictures or make color copies of your originals to create multiple versions of the same design. This card shown in the project has a baby motif, and it could be used to celebrate the birth of a child.

YOU WILL NEED

Pencil
Brown parcel paper,
   8 × 8cm
Fine felt-tipped pen
Black water-soluble
   marker pen
Garden water spray
Gold marker pen
Cream card, 20 × 16cm
Clear, all-purpose
   adhesive

154

3. Use a water spray to mist over the picture with water. The image will "bleed" around the edges. Dab off any excess water with a paper towel, then leave to dry for about 20 minutes.

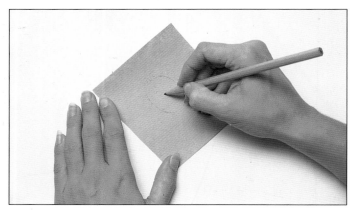

1. Draw the design in pencil on the brown paper, tracing the template here if you are not confident of your artistic skills. Go over the lines with a fine black pen.

4. Add any further decoration with a gold marker pen.

2. Draw a frame around the design, then fill in the area between the frame and the design with a black water-soluble marker pen.

5. Trim to size, then glue directly to the front of a folded piece of cream card.

PRESENT PERFECT

Pop-up boxes are especially pleasing to make because, unlike other techniques, they fully enclose a space to create a real sense of volume. The lid pieces need to be accurately cut so that the top closes fully. The grid is drawn to a scale of 1:2.

YOU WILL NEED

Backing sheet (thin
    textured gray card
    glued to mounting
    card), 28 × 16cm
Adhesive tape
Thick yellow and red card
    (for box and ribbons), a
    total of about 30 × 15cm
Scissors
Craft knife or scalpel
Clear, all-purpose
    adhesive

156

KEY

——————— cut along this line

——————— mountain crease

glue here (sometimes
on the underside)

Bows

Box

1. Cut the backing sheet in half, place it face down, butt the cut edges together, and stick them together with tape so that it will lie flat after being folded. Use the template (LEFT) to cut out the box and ribbons. Apply glue to the underside of the bows, position them on the box and glue them in place.

2. Crease the box as shown and add glue to the end tab.

3. Fold and make a square tube.

4. Apply glue to each lid tab in turn. The photograph shows the outer face of a tab being glued, so that the tab lies inside the box. However, if the inner face is glued, so that the tab lies outside the box, the pop-up has more strength and will not burst. The disadvantage is that the tab will be seen. So decide which is best for your card.

6. Glue the box to the backing sheet.

5. Glue the underside of the tabs at the base of the box. Note that the tabs are folded inwards.

7. This shows how the pop-up box closes. Note how the lid pieces separate.

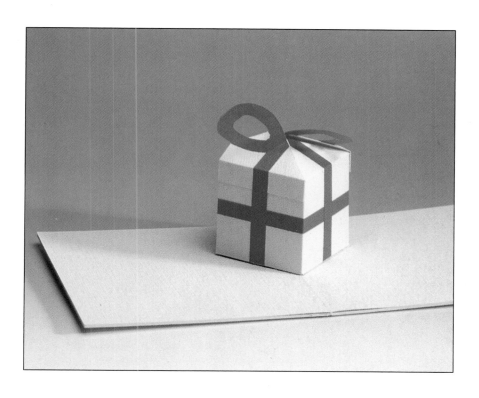

A SLICE OF CAKE

If you use reflective card for the backing sheet, the completed card will make it look as if there are several slices of cake. The folds must be accurately marked and creased if the card is to open smoothly. The grid is drawn to a scale of 1:2.

YOU WILL NEED

Backing sheet (thick
    mirror card), 26 × 16cm
Adhesive tape
Thin white card (for cake),
    20 × 15cm
Felt-tipped pens
Scissors
Craft knife or scalpel
Clear, all-purpose
    adhesive

158

1. Cut the backing sheet in half, place it face down, butt the cut edges together, and stick them together with tape so that it will lie flat after being folded. Use the template (BELOW) to cut out the cake. Cut two slits in the backing sheet.

2. Fold the decorated cake along the lines and glue the tab on the point of the cake wedge to make the cake three-dimensional.

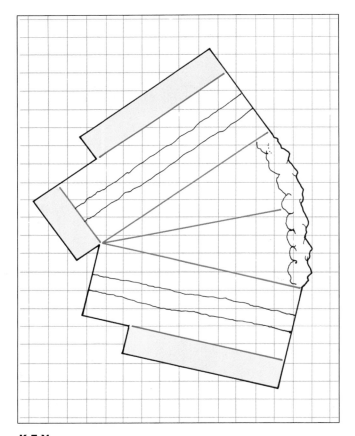

KEY

▬▬▬	cut along this line
▬▬▬	suggested artwork
▬▬▬	mountain crease
▬▬▬	valley crease
▭	glue here (sometimes on the underside)

3. Push the tabs along the bottom of the cake through the slits in the backing sheet.

4. They should fit through them like this.

5. Use adhesive tape to hold the tabs flat on the reverse of the backing sheet.

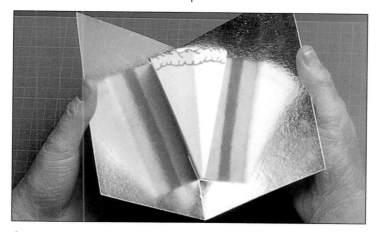

6. The cake complete. Reflective card will make this slice of cake appear to be many.

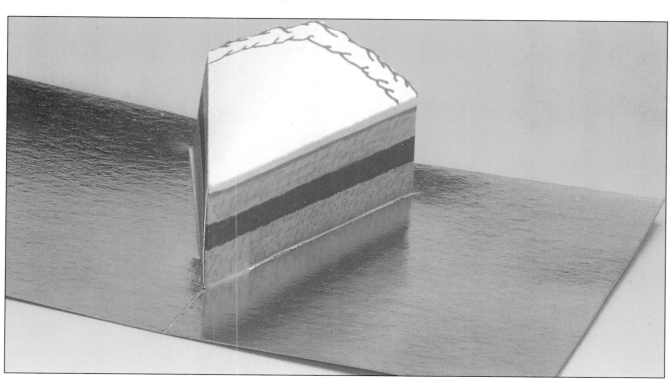

INDIAN IDEAS

Presents to celebrate a special occasion often call for something a little out of the ordinary, and here are some ideas based on the vibrant colors and intricate decorations of India. Some specialist stores stock exquisite silks, ribbons, and accessories, and you should also look out for tassels, little fabric birds, and metal ornaments.

Marbled papers are widely available, but you can easily make your own version at home. Simply fill a large plastic dish, about 6cm deep, with thin wallpaper paste. Mix two or three colors of oil paint with mineral spirit until they are of a medium consistency. Drop spots of color on the paste and gently stir with a knitting needle. Place the paper carefully on the surface of the oil, lift it out, and leave to dry.

More in keeping with the exotic theme, however, are glowing foils and metallic papers, colored silk tassels, and little metal charms and trinkets. These irresistible parcels are finished off with rather unusual tags.

160

YOU WILL NEED

Medium weight paper
Scissors
Selection of candy
    wrappers

Sequins
Clear, all-purpose adhesive
Ribbon or sewing thread

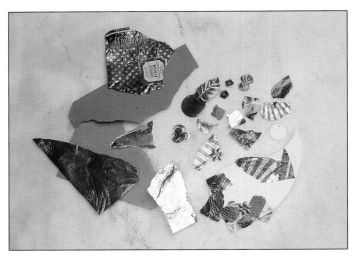

2. Use adhesive to cover the tag with small, torn pieces of candy wrappers and sequins.

1. Cut out from the paper the shape of the tag. Do not just use rectangles or squares – these tags can be any shape you want.

3. Trim away the excess from around the edges of the tag and punch a hole in the top. Thread through some fine ribbon or several strands of colorful cotton.

RIGHT: You will find a wide selection of ornaments and tags for decorating your Indian-style gifts. The colored paper labels were, in fact, made from candy wrappers, but the other ornaments were sold as Christmas decorations.

161

ABOVE: When you have wrapped your gift in a single, bright color, tie it with metallic or brightly colored silk ribbons, and add some tassels or little fabric birds.

ABOVE: Wrap a narrow strip of hand-marbled paper around a bought paper bag and decorate it with beads and metal charms, threaded on lengths of cotton.

VALENTINE'S DAY

The heart is a symbol of love and friendship. Heart images can be used on gifts for many different occasions – Mother's Day, a wedding, a christening, and so on – but most often on Valentine's Day. Hearts can be very decorative or simple, symmetrical, or more stylized. On the following pages are some inspirational ideas, ranging from a simple heart-shaped box with a handmade tag to wire hearts threaded with flowers. Look out for old, heart-shaped boxes and containers that can be repainted and decorated.

HEART-SHAPED BAG

This decorative heart-shaped bag is deceptively simple to make. The design is based on a semicircle, and it can be made from many different types of paper or card. It is easy to alter the size – just make sure that the angles are the same as those shown.

YOU WILL NEED

Sheet of card or paper
Pair of compasses
Pencil
Ruler
Protractor
Scissors
Glue stick

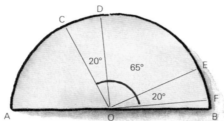

2. Mark another point, 20° from C, then another at 65° and another at 20°. Join all these points at the center.

4. Cut out the whole shape and score all lines from the center out to the edge. Fold. Glue the shaded area to the heart shape.

BELOW: Punch holes in the side panels of the heart-shaped bag and make handles. You can either use colored card for the bag, or make it in plain paper and decorate it as you wish.

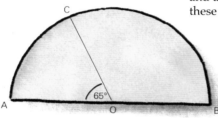

1. Draw a semicircle and make a point about 65° from one edge (C).

3. Now divide both of the largest arcs in half, either by measuring or using a protractor. Draw semicircles on each half.

GINGERBREAD

They say that the way to the heart is through the stomach, so these gingerbread figures are an unusual but appropriate addition to these little gift bags. Use dried cranberries, bay leaves, and chiles for extra decorations. The red bag has been decorated with a large paper bow, with the bay leaves, raffia, and gingerbread, while chiles and bay leaves have been added to the purple and light brown bag. An easy alternative would be to thread dried cranberries onto some wire, which could then be bent into a heart shape and tied to the gingerbread.

YOU WILL NEED

75g soft brown sugar	½ tsp baking soda
2 tbsp golden syrup	200g plain flour
1 tbsp molasses	1 tsp ground ginger
2 tbsp water	1 tsp cinnamon
100g butter	

1. Bring the sugar, syrup, molasses, and water to a boil, stirring well.

2. Remove the pan from the heat and stir in the butter and baking soda. Stir in the flour and spices, and mix together well.

3. Leave the dough for 1 hour. Pre-heat the oven to 180°C/Gas Mark 4. Roll out the dough on a floured board until it is about 0.4cm thick. Cut out the gingerbread shapes and lay on a buttered baking tray.

4. Bake for 10–12 minutes. Pierce holes for hanging while the gingerbread is still warm, and leave to cool on a wire tray.

165

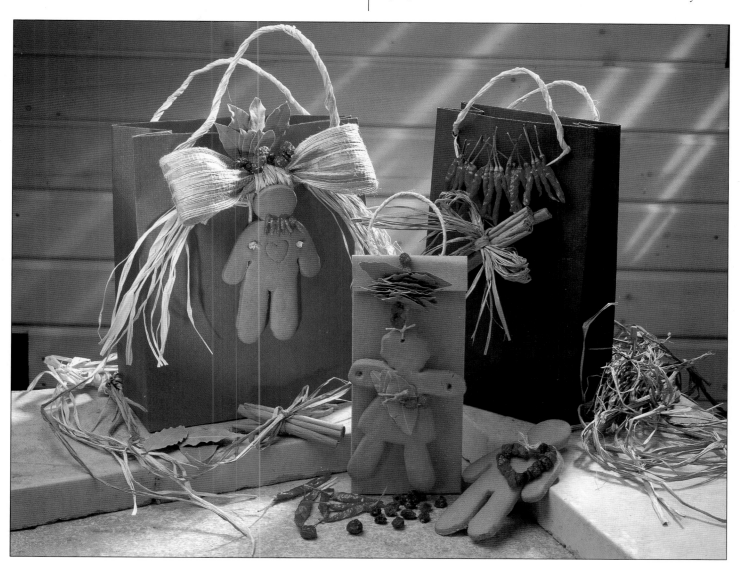

FABRIC COLLAGE

Red hearts are an obvious choice for a Valentine's Day card when you want to show someone how much you care. This easy-to-make card uses scraps of fabric, in shades of pink, red, and orange, and the gold has been added to give a rich, luxurious effect.

YOU WILL NEED

White sugar paper
Pencil
Scissors
Small pieces of red and
   pink felt fabric, about
   15 × 15cm
Cotton wool or wadding

Needle and sewing threads
   to match fabrics
Gold and woven patterned
   fabrics
Clear, all-purpose adhesive
White card, about 20 × 15cm

166

1. Draw a heart shape on a piece of paper and use it as a template. Cut a heart shape from a piece of pink felt.

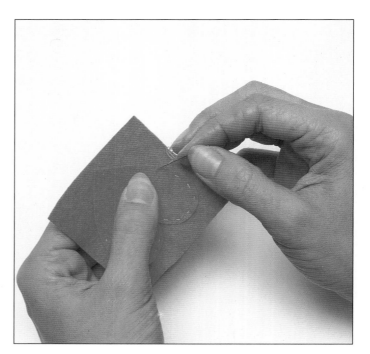

2. Place the heart on a background fabric of a different color and stitch it in place with a simple running stitch. Do not sew all the way round the heart, but leave a gap of about 2cm.

3. Push a small amount of cotton wool through the gap to pad the heart, then sew up the opening. This will give the heart a slightly three-dimensional effect.

4. Select a larger piece of a contrasting fabric to back the felt to which the heart is stitched. Cut it to size and stitch them together.

5. If you are using a fine fabric, like the gold one shown, carefully fray the edges to give a decorative effect. As a border, repeat the felt used for the heart. Cut the fabric to size and glue it to the frayed fabric.

167

6. Glue the whole collage to a larger piece of felt to form a background. Leave to dry for 50–60 minutes.

7. When the glue is dry, glue the completed collage to a larger, contrasting piece of folded card.

168

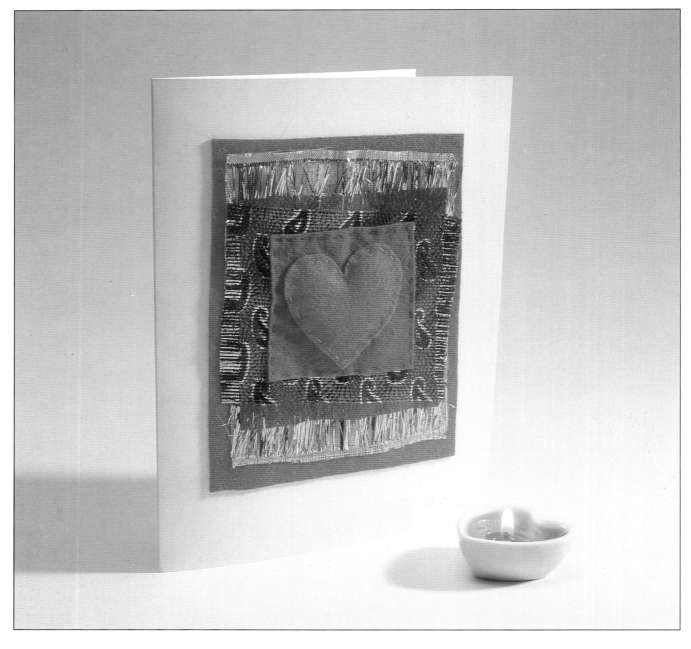

FLOWERS AND LEAVES

It has become customary to exchange cards on Valentine's Day, and giving a card that you have made yourself makes the gesture even more personal. Use the flowers and leaves from your garden or from the hedgerows to make your Valentine's card by pressing them, backing them with thin card, then mounting them on colored, fine-corrugated card. Ivy leaves form a charming and natural heart shape – a single leaf could have a little heart cut from it or you could arrange a group of leaves into a pretty heart. Pansies are the symbols of thoughts, and are the most appropriate of flowers to indicate that you are thinking of someone.

YOU WILL NEED

Fresh pansies and ivy leaves
Flower press
Colored corrugated card
Craft knife
Double-sided adhesive tape
PVA adhesive
Plain paper
Sharp scissors
Adhesive pads (optional)

At least two weeks before you want to make the cards, press the flowers so that they have time to dry thoroughly. Use a flower press or put the flowers and leaves between pieces of tissue paper and place them inside a telephone directory. Place a weight on top and leave completely undisturbed in a warm, dry place for at least 10 days.

2. To make the pansy ring or the heart of ivy leaves, glue the pressed flowers or leaves to plain paper in the arrangement of your choice. When the adhesive is dry, use a craft knife or sharp pointed scissors to cut around the shapes. Attach the cut-out shape to the front of the card with adhesive or, if you want a slightly three-dimensional effect, with adhesive pads.

1. To make the ivy leaf card, take a rectangle of corrugated card, and fold it in half. Cut out a square window in the front. Use double-sided tape or adhesive to glue the paper behind the window. Glue the leaf to the paper, and use a craft knife to cut out a tiny heart in the leaf and then cut around the leaf so that the plain paper falls away. Remember that sections of the leaf must be attached to the card frame on all sides.

CUPID'S ARROW

There is a certain elegance when a supporting tab becomes part of the design of a pop-up card. In this case, the tab that supports the heart has become the arrow. Thus, no part of the design is superfluous. Note also how the arrow slides through the heart when the card is opened. The technique of piercing one pop-up shape with another need not be confined to a large shape and a thin one. Any shape can pierce another, thus eliminating the need for extra supporting tabs. The grid is drawn to a scale of 1:2.

YOU WILL NEED

Backing sheet (thin glossy
　yellow card), 36 × 11cm
Thin red card (for heart),
　13 × 13cm
Thin blue card (for arrow),
　15 × 4cm
Scalpel
Clear, all-purpose
　adhesive

Heart

Flight

Arrow

1. Cut the backing sheet in half, place it face down, butt the cut edges together, and stick with tape so that they will lie flat after being folded. Cut out the pieces, using the template (LEFT). Apply glue to the heart tab.

2. Glue the tab to the backing sheet so that the crease in the backing sheet lies approximately behind the center line of the heart.

KEY

▬▬▬	cut along this line
┈┈┈	suggested artwork
▬▬▬	mountain crease
▬▬▬	valley crease
▭	glue here (sometimes on the underside)

3. Feed the arrow through the slit in the heart from right to left.

4. Glue the end of the arrow to the backing sheet.

5. Glue the flight to the end of the arrow.

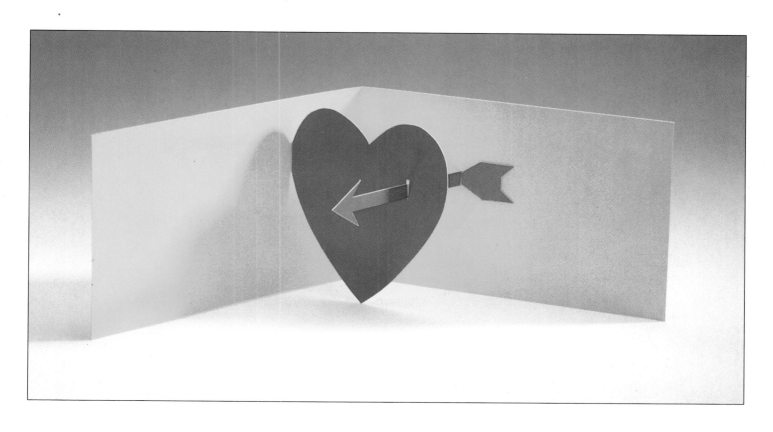

TRUE LOVE

This is one of the simplest pop-up cards you could make. Note how the paper is folded behind to create a double thickness that prevents the design from buckling. This also means that the design can be made from paper, rather than card. The grid is drawn to a scale of 1:2½.

YOU WILL NEED
Medium weight red paper, 26 × 20cm
Scalpel

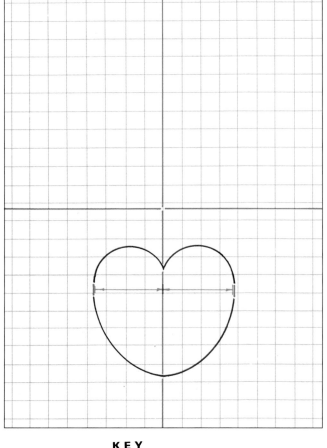

KEY

▬▬ cut along this line

▬▬ mountain crease

▬▬ valley crease

1. Draw half of the heart shape as shown, onto the paper. Fold the sheet in half, not through the heart. Then fold it in half again.

2. Open the sheet out. Note the position of the half-heart.

3. Cut out the heart, being careful to leave the small sections uncut that are marked to be folded on the template.

4. Fold back the heart to create these creases.

5. Reform the folds, and pull up the hearts, creating a mountain fold down the center of the heart.

Dress up some simple boxes with a few personal touches. Decorate plain ribbon with fabric relief paint and make your own tags. Cut out a large heart outline and a smaller pierced heart, and tie them on with raffia.

HEARTS HAVE IT

Decorate a large sheet of paper with a simple pattern of stenciled hearts — nothing could be simpler, and you can make a gift tag to match and finish it off with some pretty curls of ribbon. Do not worry if the stenciled images do not fit perfectly within the edges of the paper. When you wrap up your gift, you may end up cutting off some of the design.

YOU WILL NEED

Scrap paper
Ruler and pencil
Heart-shaped stencil
Acrylic or stencil paint
Saucer or palette
Stencil brush
Large sheet of red poster
    paper

174

1. On a piece of scrap paper, work out several versions of a grid so that the hearts will be evenly spaced over the paper.

2. Try out a variety of arrangements, spacing the hearts in diagonal patterns or straight lines.

3. When you are happy with the arrangement, plot the same grid on the poster paper. Use very light pencil dots – they should be just dark enough for you to see them as a guide for positioning the stencil but not so dark that they will detract from your design.

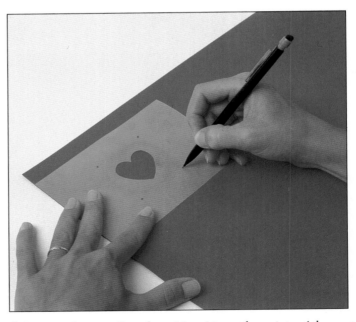

4. Position the stencil on the grid and trace the points of the paper grid onto the stencil using a pencil or permanent marker. This will make it easy for you to position the stencil accurately every time by simply matching the dots.

5. Now stencil the wrapping paper. Make sure that the brush is absolutely clean before you begin, and remember to remove excess paint on a paper towel.

6. As you work, try to make sure that the images are all more or less the same density. Do not try to match them perfectly, however, because the slight differences add to the charm.

175

LEFT: Make some original gift-wrap paper by stenciling white hearts onto some shop-bought red paper. Make a matching red and white tag, and tie the parcel with white paper ribbon. For a special treat, add a chocolate heart.

PIERCED PAPER

The technique of piercing paper can be used for gift wrap, tags, ribbons, and cards. The delicate effect is achieved by piercing the paper with the fine point of a needle or nail. Although hearts have been used here, any simple motif would be equally effective.

YOU WILL NEED

Acetate or oiled parchment
   for stencils
Scalpel

Colored paper:
   2 contrasting shades
Needles: 2 different sizes

176

1. Prepare stencils for two hearts, making them different sizes. Cut out a heart of each size from the colored paper.

2. Lay the hearts on a soft blanket or something similar, and pierce around the edge of the larger heart with the thicker point.

3. Repeat the process with the smaller heart and finer needle. Pierce a hole through the top of each heart, and thread through a ribbon.

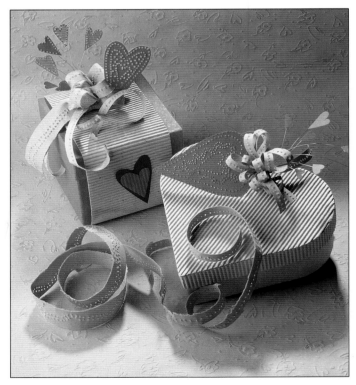

ABOVE: Wrap boxes in corrugated card and decorate with pierced paper, ribbon, and tags. Glue some small hearts to pieces of wire and gather them into a bunch to decorate a gift.

PLEATED PAPER

Pleating is a versatile but simple technique, and sections of pleated paper make wonderful gift wraps. Use lightweight paper that can be easily folded. Vary the depths of the pleats and the width of the paper to get different effects, but keep the pleats even and the creases sharp. White, textured, handmade papers look particularly effective. The delicate pleating used on these gifts is reminiscent of Japanese papercraft.

YOU WILL NEED

Sufficient paper to wrap the gift plus a piece twice the length of the parcel
Double-sided adhesive tape

1. Cut a piece of paper about twice the length of the wrapped box. Begin folding over the width of the pleat you require. Make a narrow strip of pleated paper and a very small section for the matching tag.

2. Secure the wide piece of pleated paper at one end. Gently twist the paper until the desired effect is achieved, then stick down the other end. Add the narrower pleated strip in the same way.

MOTHER'S DAY

The art of wrapping and the art of giving could be said to be one and the same. A beautifully wrapped box shows that you have chosen and wrapped the gift it contains with equal care.

Remember to always choose your wrapping paper with care and to fold it neatly, using double-sided tape to ensure neat edges.

The decorative ribbons you use should start and end at the point where the join will be hidden under a bow or a gift tag.

A carefully selected ribbon can turn a plainly wrapped parcel into an attractively wrapped present, while a pretty bow, perhaps combined with silk or ribbon flowers, will transform it into a sensational gift.

SAY IT WITH FLOWERS

This is a simple design in technical terms, but it is very decoratively versatile. The specific shapes of the vase, foliage, and blooms can be varied as you prefer – try roses, tulips, or pansies. The colors shown here are, of course, only suggestions.
The grid is drawn to a scale of 1:2½.

YOU WILL NEED

Backing sheet (white
   mounting card),
   48 × 23cm
Double-sided adhesive
   tape
Scalpel

Felt tipped pens
Thick watercolor paper
   (for flowers and vase),
   46 × 25cm
Clear, all-purpose
   adhesive

180

Back layer

Front layer

KEY

———	cut along this line
········	suggested artwork
———	mountain crease
▭	glue here (sometimes on the underside)
—— ——	these measurements are the same

Vase

Support

1. Cut the backing sheet in half, place it face down, butt the cut edges together, and stick them together with tape so that it will lie flat after being folded. Cut out the pieces.

2. Apply glue to the right-hand edge of the support and glue it to the backing sheet.

3. Apply glue to the base of the back layer of flowers.

4. Slot it into the first slit in the support (that nearer the backing sheet) and fix the tab to the backing sheet.

5. Repeat the previous step for the front layer of flowers.

6. Glue the vase to the front of the support to complete the structure.

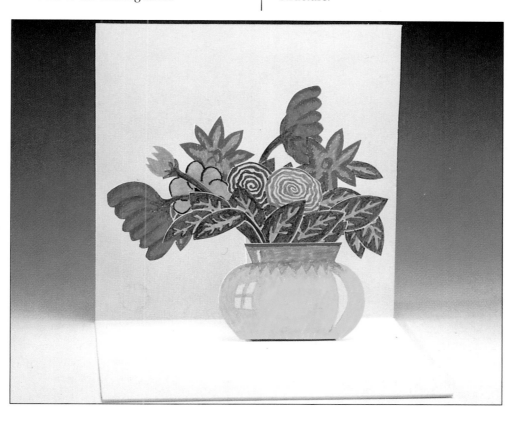

THREE-DIMENSIONAL POSY

This elegant card is easy to make with a rubber stamp and some embossing powder. Embossing is a simple technique that gives some really unusual, eye-catching results, but it can be disappointing if it is not done correctly. The embossing powder has to be heated, and the easiest tool to use is a hand-held paint stripper. However, you can achieve the same results with an iron, a hot plate, or even a hot light bulb. The powdered image has to be heated until the powder melts, but it is important that the image is held near to, but does not touch, the heat source. Do not over-heat the image or it will appear flat and waxy.

YOU WILL NEED

Orange card, 21 × 15cm
Burgundy card, 14 × 9cm
Clear, all-purpose
  adhesive
Cream card, 14 × 9cm
Floral wreath stamp
Embossing ink pad

Gold embossing powder
Heat source
Felt-tipped pens: pink,
  cranberry, purple, yellow,
  green
Craft knife or scalpel
Self-adhesive pads

---

1. Place the burgundy card on the orange card and glue in position.

2. Ink the stamp and print two wreaths on the cream card. While the images are still wet, pour embossing powder over them. Shake to remove the excess powder. Heat the images until the powder melts, which will take 15–20 seconds, depending on the strength of your heat source.

3. Color one wreath completely, using felt-tipped pens. On the second wreath, color in only the purple flowers.

4. Carefully cut out the colored wreath and place it to one side. From the second wreath, cut out the purple flowers.

5. Position the complete wreath on the burgundy card and stick it down.

183

6. Cut self-adhesive pads in half or even quarters. Use them to position the individual flowers over their counterparts in the full wreath.

PLEASING PASTELS

Lightweight paper can be used to make flowers and leaves. Pierce holes in the center of simple flower shapes and thread them onto 2.5cm of rolled-up paper. Glue them to the gift with some paper leaves. You can make simple tags with coordinating papers, all of a similar weight, cut with pinking shears, glued together, and with holes punched in the corners. Decorate them with small flowers. This simple gift of stationery has been made extra special by wrapping decorative strips of colored paper around the central bands. Add a pencil or ball-point pen, decorated to look like a flower or a leaf, to make a simple gift special.

184

YOU WILL NEED

Lightweight papers in the
  colors of your choice
Pinking shears
Scissors
Pencil or ball-point pen
Double-sided adhesive
  tape
Glue stick

1. Cut several strips of colored paper, cutting patterns along the edge. Use pinking shears to give a zigzag edge to one side of the strips. Wrap these around the gift. Wrap a pencil or pen in green paper.

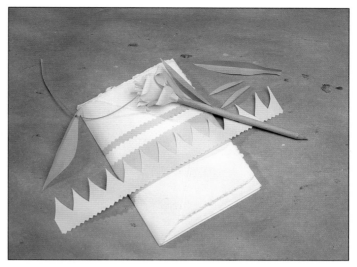

2. Cut out several petal shapes in paper and curl over the edges by pulling them over the blade of your scissors. Cut a rectangle of paper and make a series of cuts into one side. Wrap the paper around the top of the pencil, and curl back the strips slightly to form the center of the flower. Add some larger petals around the edge.

3. Cut some leaf shapes and glue them to the pencil. Cut a leaf shape for the tag and attach it to the gift with a thin strip of paper.

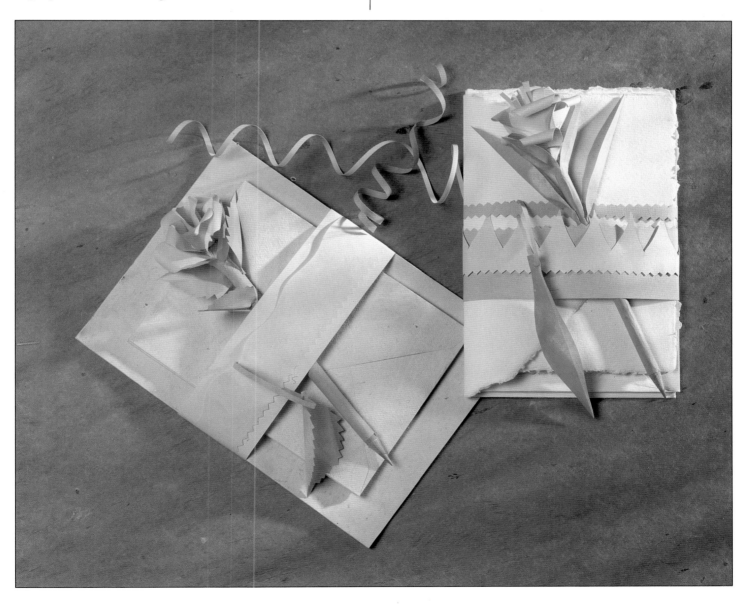

PAISLEY PATTERN PAPER

This striking wrapping paper has been very simply made – it is just tissue paper decorated with a simple paisley-type stamp. Instead of the silver pigment ink, you could use white, but the silver gives a pretty, shimmery effect, which is complemented by the metallic ribbon.

YOU WILL NEED

Sheet of turquoise tissue   Silver pigment ink pad
    paper   Floral paisley stamp

186

1. Cut the paper to fit the parcel. If you cut it slightly larger than needed, you can hold the paper flat on your work top with small pieces of masking tape in the corners. Ink the stamp and print a row of the motifs, all facing the same way. Re-ink the stamp between each impression. Leave a space of about 4cm and print a second row, with the motif facing the same way. Repeat the process until you have reached the end of the paper.

2. Turn the stamp upside down, and print further rows, positioning the motifs evenly in the spaces between the existing rows.

3. Wait until the ink has dried before wrapping the parcel.

PRESSED HERB POSTCARDS

*Greeting cards made from pressed flowers, herbs, and spices are always appreciated,
particularly if the plants that you use have a special meaning.*

YOU WILL NEED

Selection of fresh herbs,
  such as sage, thyme,
  marjoram, parsley,
  tarragon or rosemary
Flower press or telephone
  directory

Paintbrush
PVA glue
Small rectangles of hand-
  made rag paper

---

1. Select the best sprigs from each herb and press them in a flower press or a telephone directory for at least two weeks. When dry, remove from the press or telephone directory very carefully otherwise you could damage the delicate leaves.

2. Using a small paintbrush, paste glue onto the herb sprig and carefully press onto the rag paper backing.

THE LANGUAGE OF HERBS AND SPICES

In days gone by, when messages were often exchanged and thoughts were expressed without a word being written or spoken, the giving and receiving of a small herbal posy could secretly transmit the deepest sentiments. For your card, choose the herb or spice which best expresses your feelings.

188

Allspice	compassion
Angelica	inspiration
Basil, sweet	good wishes
Bay leaf	forever constant
Bay tree	glory
Camomile	energy in adversity
Chervil	sincerity
Cilantro	dignity
Cloves	concealed merit
Fennel	force, strength

Camomile

Thyme

Pink

Southernwood

Pink, clove	enduring sweetness
Rose, cabbage	ambassador of love
Rose, moss	superior merit
Saffron crocus	mirth
Sage	esteem, domestic virtue
Sorrel	parental affection
Southernwood	jest, bantering
Spearmint	warmth of sentiment
Tarragon	lasting interest
Thyme	activity, courage

Frankincense	a faithful heart
Geranium, nutmeg	unexpected meeting
Juniper	succour, protection
Lady's mantle	fashion
Lavender	industry
Mint	virtue
Myrrh	gladness
Oregano	substance
Parsley	festivity
Peppermint	warmth, cordiality

Oregano

Parsley

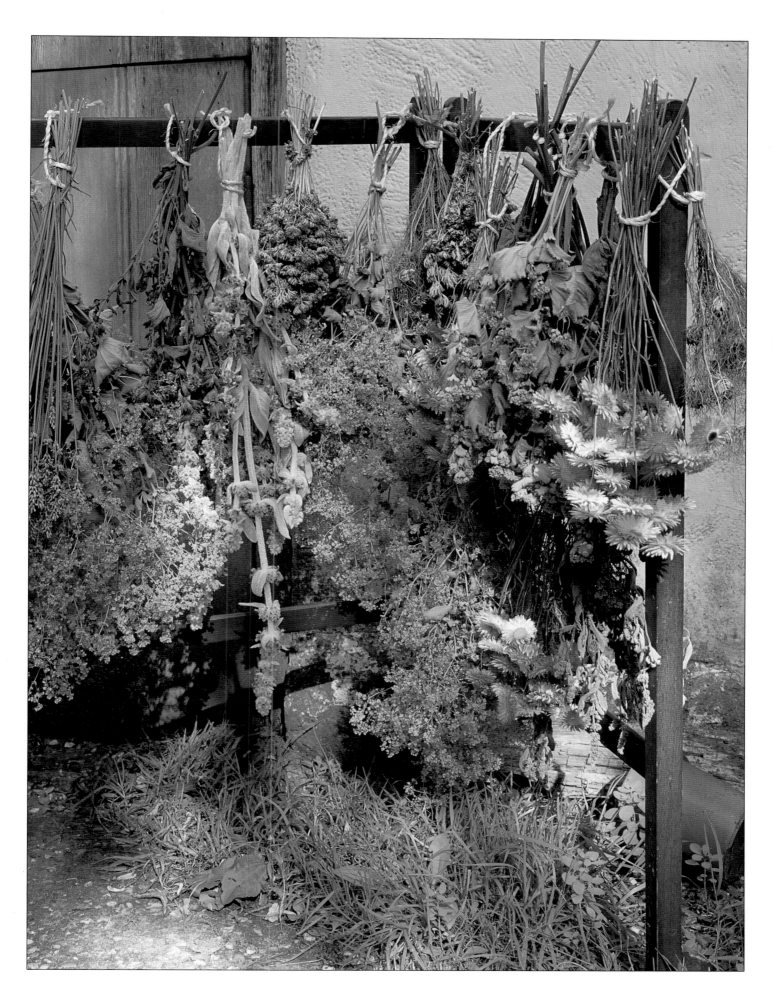

SPICE BALLS

These beautiful and fragrant spice balls make a colorful and exotic addition to any gift – not just for Mother's Day, of course, but they would be a lovely adornment on a special gift. Fill a plain brown box with a selection of cooking spices or pot pourri, tie the box with natural colored raffia, and attach a spice ball.

YOU WILL NEED

Florist's stub wires	Sunflower seeds
Polystyrene ball	Dried corn kernels
Snub-nosed pliers	Raffia
Clear, all-purpose adhesive	Dried bay leaves

190

1. Push a length of wire right through a polystyrene ball and use pliers to turn a loop in the end. Draw a spiral of glue around the ball and carefully stick on the sunflower seeds.

2. When the glue has dried, draw a second spiral and stick on the kernels. Leave until the glue is dry.

3. Thread some raffia through the loop on the base of the ball. Trim the wire if necessary at the other end, and turn another loop. Tie on some more raffia and add an extra length for fastening the spice ball to the parcel. Glue on some bay leaves to finish.

INDEX